The Virtue of Playfulness

This book argues that in order for people to live well, they must develop a virtue of playfulness. Inspired by Aristotle, the book draws on work from philosophy, classics, history, biology, psychology, and media studies to understand the place of play and playfulness in a good life.

Many philosophers have written about play, from Presocratics such as Heraclitus to contemporary philosophers such as Bernard Suits. Some champion play as the most crucial value in life. Others deride it and warn strongly against it. This book evaluates the research on how play and playfulness bear on living a good life and becoming a good person. Its main argument is that in order to understand play as an action, we must understand playfulness as a virtue in the lives of good people. The author develops a theory of playfulness from an Aristotelian perspective. Like Aristotle sees the virtues as necessary for a happy life, the author argues that playfulness is necessary for living well. And just as Aristotle offers multifaceted characterizations of core virtues, the author argues that playfulness includes aspects of seriousness, creativity, humility, optimism, and sociality. Playful people take play seriously, learn new skills, overcome failure, strive for success, and keep others in mind. As a result, playful people have a better shot at living well.

The Virtue of Playfulness is an accessible, empirically informed, and detailed treatment of the philosophy of playfulness. It will appeal to scholars and students in philosophy and related disciplines who are interested in virtue ethics, moral psychology, philosophy of games, philosophy of sport, and ancient philosophy.

boomer trujillo is assistant professor of instruction in the Department of Philosophy at the University of Texas at El Paso. His thought is captured in articles like "The Friends of Sisyphus," "Stoicism Sucks," "The Benefits of Being a Suicidal Curmudgeon," and "Friendship for the Flawed."

Routledge Focus on Philosophy

Routledge Focus on Philosophy is an exciting and innovative new series, capturing and disseminating some of the best and most exciting new research in philosophy in short book form. Peer reviewed and at a maximum of fifty thousand words shorter than the typical research monograph, *Routledge Focus on Philosophy* titles are available in both ebook and print on demand format. Tackling big topics in a digestible format the series opens up important philosophical research for a wider audience, and as such is invaluable reading for the scholar, researcher and student seeking to keep their finger on the pulse of the discipline. The series also reflects the growing interdisciplinarity within philosophy and will be of interest to those in related disciplines across the humanities and social sciences.

Moral Choices for Our Future Selves
An Empirical Theory of Prudential Perception and a Moral Theory of Prudence
Eleonora Viganò

Moralistics and Psychomoralistics
A Unified Cognitive Science of Moral Intuition
Graham Wood

Idealism after Existentialism
Encounters in Philosophy of Religion
N.N. Trakakis

State Secrecy and Democracy
A Philosophical Inquiry
Dorota Mokrosinska

The Virtue of Playfulness
Why Happy People are Playful
boomer trujillo

For more information about this series, please visit: www.routledge.com/Routledge-Focus-on-Philosophy/book-series/RFP

"In this clear and fun to read book, boomer trujillo convincingly shows that playfulness is a virtue necessary for the good life. *The Virtue of Playfulness* is an important contribution to the growing work on the importance of play and its role in our lives."

Shawn E. Klein, *Arizona State University, USA*

"This is a serious and scholarly consideration of the nature, virtue and importance of play and playfulness. trujillo provides an Aristotelian reading of play as part of a flourishing and worthwhile life and rightly concludes that life is best lived playfully."

Emily Ryall, *University of Gloucestershire, UK*

"*The Virtue of Playfulness* is a timely, erudite, and compelling inquiry into the nature and importance of the virtue of playfulness. trujillo impressively and insightfully draws on work across the wide spectrum and deep history of philosophy, while deftly noting the scientific import of his claims. Despite the complexity of his subject and the breadth of his sources, trujillo's writing is lucid, engaging, and frequently witty. At a time when philosophers are finally exploring play and its kin in more detail—through the investigation of spontaneous freedom, games, volitional openness, and art—trujillo's focus on playfulness as a virtue makes an exciting contribution."

Nick Riggle, *The University of San Diego, USA*

"boomer trujillo's book, *The Virtue of Playfulness: Why Happy People Are Playful*, is a must-read for anyone interested in playfulness, moral virtue, the good life, or simply human nature. For context, I am writing a book on the nature and value of playfulness myself, and I not only have read boomer's wonderful book draft from cover to cover carefully twice, gleaning substantial new insights each time; I also have devoted the better part of a chapter to explaining why I disagree with him. I am sure I will read it from cover to cover again many more times; it richly repays careful study, and I plan to use it in my teaching. There can be no doubt that trujillo's theory of playfulness is now the 'theory to beat.' It is also written in a very accessible and engaging style, and I recommend it enthusiastically."

Michael Ridge, *The University of Edinburgh, UK*

"We know that 'all work and no play makes Jack a dull boy,' but too many philosophers have scorned play as time wasted, or else have valued it unreflectively as the mere absence of work. What if, instead, there are distinctive goods of play, and both mental and physical skills through which we can do a better or worse job of playing? This sounds paradoxical: doing a better job of playing? But boomer trujillo's eudaimonistic account of the virtue of playfulness and its essential role in a good life approaches this challenge with wisdom and seriousness, effectively making the case that playfulness belongs in an Aristotelian system. trujillo's appropriately light touch and lucid prose make this book an important contribution to the literature in eudaimonistic ethics, the philosophy of play, sport, and games, as well as an excellent introduction to virtue ethics for students at all levels."

Avery Kolers, *The University of Louisville, USA*

The Virtue of Playfulness
Why Happy People Are Playful

boomer trujillo

First published 2024
by Routledge
605 Third Avenue, New York, NY 10158

and by Routledge
4 Park Square, Milton Park, Abingdon, Oxon, OX14 4RN

Routledge is an imprint of the Taylor & Francis Group, an informa business

© 2024 boomer trujillo

The right of boomer trujillo to be identified as author of this work has been asserted in accordance with sections 77 and 78 of the Copyright, Designs and Patents Act 1988.

All rights reserved. No part of this book may be reprinted or reproduced or utilised in any form or by any electronic, mechanical, or other means, now known or hereafter invented, including photocopying and recording, or in any information storage or retrieval system, without permission in writing from the publishers.

Trademark notice: Product or corporate names may be trademarks or registered trademarks, and are used only for identification and explanation without intent to infringe.

ISBN: 978-1-032-71774-6 (hbk)
ISBN: 978-1-032-71773-9 (pbk)
ISBN: 978-1-032-71772-2 (ebk)

DOI: 10.4324/9781032717722

Typeset in Times New Roman
SPi Technologies India Pvt Ltd (Straive)

To my leisure-time companions—the bloods and buds, the memers and dreamers and streamers

Contents

Acknowledgments   *x*
Abbreviations of Aristotle's Works   *xii*

Introduction: Playfulness, Seriously   1

1 Aristotle on Play as Medicine   9

2 Aristotle on Being Happy, Virtuous, and (Maybe) Playful   29

3 Harmonizing the Cacophony of Claims about Play   43

4 The Virtue of Playfulness   63

Conclusion: Happy People Play, Playful People Live   93

References   *95*
Index   *106*

Acknowledgments

It is a struggle for me not to let the perfect be the enemy of the good. This book is imperfect, but I hope that imperfect actuality is better than perfect fantasy. Imperfect words like mine carry risk. I therefore owe two parties immediate acknowledgment. First is you, reader, for taking a chance on my words. Your leisure means a lot to me, and I hope this project is worth your time. Second, I owe Routledge, Andrew Weckenmann, and Rosaleah Stammler. This book is a mishmash of disciplines and ideas, and they supported its publication. I have no book without an audience or publisher. So, thank you.

I started playing with these ideas in 2017 as a doctoral student at Vanderbilt University. Two things were immensely helpful: the Taking Play Seriously workshop that I led with Derek Price at the Robert Penn Warren Center for the Humanities, and the 2017 and 2019 Three Minute Thesis competitions where I had one slide, three minutes, and zero jargon to explain my research to non-specialists. These were the beginnings of my explaining playfulness. Eventually, I completed a dissertation on this topic in 2019. From Vanderbilt, I moved to The University of Louisville and The University of Texas at El Paso and kept revising my work. During these years, John Lachs, Jeffrey Tlumak, Scott F. Aikin, Avery Kolers, John Gibson, Andreas Elpidorou, Noah Greenstein, Shane McInnis, Michael Ridge, and Noell Birondo provided feedback on the manuscript and tips for publishing it. So did three anonymous reviewers via Routledge. This is my first book, and it would not have been finished without them.

In addition to dialectical and geographic moves on my part, American culture moved too, through COVID and protests for social justice. Writing about playfulness, as well as its ethical and social dimensions, took on grave meanings given this background. I wondered whether my healthcare friends would survive the pandemic. I heard the National Guard and Louisville Police shoot tear gas canisters and pepper balls at protestors, and I saw waves of Central and South Americans seek refuge in the United States. That was the everyday background of this book. My playfulness kept me sane(ish), locked in as I was, living as I did (and am) in cities with brutal histories of violence toward minorities. My online communities became crucial, especially on Twitch. And after lockdown, my IRL communities shared the burden, especially those at St. James, Sunergos, and Vyable, as well as local art and hardcore punk scenes in each city. My ideas about playfulness and leisure were tested in the living in these places and with their people. Specific people, though, taught me profound lessons, especially Thomas Tilton, Jorge Granados, Ruby Ann Ganal, Julián González, Patricio Reynaga, Kurt Brandner, Caden and Priscilla Cox, Jon Henry, James Ireland, Clayton Beaman, Matthew McConnell, Yiran Zhang, Robert Engelman, Hillary Parsley, Joe and Melissa Williams, Austin Boulter, Pauli Lanzetta, Clarence Kasko, Mario Rewers, Alyssa Lowery, Sabeen Ahmed, Sebastian Ramirez, Fiacha and Sarah Heneghan, Emily Meffert, Rachel Pigg, F. D. Yates, and Diana Marely Nolasco Molina. In many ways, this book struggles to express the lessons they demonstrated with lucidity.

Lastly, there is Alala. She has been the only one by my side for every part of this project, living the eternal wisdom that most philosophers only talk about, modeling playfulness one tail wag at a time. It would be a shame that she cannot read this if she did not already live it.

Abbreviations of Aristotle's Works

Cat.   *Categories*
DA   *On the Soul*
EE   *Eudemian Ethics*
EN   *Nicomachean Ethics*
MM   *Magna Moralia*
Pol.   *Politics*
Rhet. *Rhetoric*
Met.   *Metaphysics*

For convenience's sake, I quote the translations in Jonathan Barnes' two-volume *Complete Works of Aristotle* by Princeton University Press. And when referring to the Greek, I use Harvard University Press's Loeb Classical Library editions, which can be accessed online via Tufts University's Perseus Digital Library.

Introduction
Playfulness, Seriously

Philosophy and the Athenian Playpen

"Plato's Academy." The term conjures images of bearded men in a flowing, white tunics, pontificating as they stroll past marble buildings. Even though many universities perpetuate this image, it is inaccurate. Ancient Greece was vibrant and playful. For example, before he wrote his dialogues and founded the Academy, Plato crushed opponents in the wrestling ring. His wrestling coach named him after his formidable stature, *platos* meaning "broad" in Greek. And this name stuck much better than "Aristocles," his original name after his grandfather.[1] Ancient Greece had philosophy and democracy, yes. But its now time-bleached statues were once painted bright colors. Processions of Dionysian revelers periodically marched through its streets while carrying penises and shouting vulgarities. Alongside the tragedies of Sophocles were the comedies of Aristophanes who wrote about farts and sex. We hearken back to Ancient Greece for its philosophy, high art, and conquests, but not much else. For whatever reason, we rarely tend to the lighter side of life in history and academic thought. I think this is a mistake. It neglects a huge part of human life. This is especially a problem for philosophy because it takes itself as "footnotes to Plato." But few allow Plato temperamental complexity and human crudity. Footnotes to Plato differ when they are attached to texts written by an alabaster statue rather than a flesh-and-blood, battle-tested, joke-loving man in a cosmopolis.

This book is not about Plato, though the points about Greek culture hold. Instead, this book summarizes and extends the ideas of Plato's most famous student: Aristotle. I chose Aristotle because his version of ethics is more complete than Plato's, and Aristotle's theory became relevant to contemporary ethics when a group of women philosophers—especially Philippa Foot, Rosalind Hursthouse, and Martha Nussbaum—revitalized his approach. They founded a "neo-Aristotelian" theory, and I subscribe to it.[2] I will not defend neo-Aristotelian virtue ethics as the best theory to hold. But I will show how it can handle subtle subjects like play and playfulness, the core ideas for this book.

I also invite ethicists of other persuasions to add to my discussion. Philosophy does best when it plays well with others. After all, when refuting Plato, Aristotle said he was a friend foremost to truth (*EN* 1096a11-18), and Marcus Aurelius openly asked for refutations because self-deceit and ignorance harm people more than the truth.[3] I agree with them. When playing philosophy, I would rather you co-create ideas with me than merely spectate. If you think that I am wrong, first, I am flattered that you are thinking of me, and second, I am happy to listen to why you think so.

This book is about taking play seriously. More precisely, it is about the virtue of playfulness. Throughout, I distinguish *play* (an action) from *playfulness* (a moral character trait). In thousands of years, few philosophers have written on playfulness as a character trait, which is why I hope to advance a theory of playfulness here.[4] I am concerned less about what constitutes an action of play and more about what playful people do, on what occasions, and in what ways. This distinction matters because someone can play (do playful things) without being playful (being a person who uses her leisure time in the right ways, in the right circumstances, consistently well across time, or so I argue). This latter phenomenon is what I hope to classify.

But when I say "classify," I do not mean to offer a genus and use differentia, a strategy Aristotle deploys in his *Metaphysics*. Nor do I hope to give precise semantic boundaries for what terms refer to, at least not to the extent that Aristotle does in *Categories*. Both are suitable ways of defining things that can be metaphysically and semantically exact. However, whatever lines the boundaries of playfulness have, they feather at the edges. I focus on playfulness's ethical dimensions, and unfortunately, this means that my definitions cannot be as precise as logic, geometry, or even biology. I heed Aristotle's advice on ethics. In ethical work, he cautions readers that truth can be offered only roughly and in outline, and no wise person ever looks for more precision in a subject than it actually allows (*EN* 1094b11-25, 1098a25-33). There is irremovable imprecision when talking about good lives, good people, and the characteristics of both, such as play and playfulness. But these theoretical limits constrain only the precision possible in this conversation, not its importance. The stakes are no more or no less than living a good life. If what I am saying has no relation to everyday action, my project failed.

So, how do I hope to offer a characterization of playfulness? I use examples and generalized descriptions of phenomena. Aristotle looks to good people who live good lives, and they become exemplars of ethical values, as well as templates for deliberation. Aristotle often works from examples, and he conceptualizes virtue as an intermediate state of proper development between extremes of malformation of character. Virtues are frequently found in the intellectual Goldilocks zone. For example, courage is facing fear in just the right way, neither being too afraid (as a coward) nor utterly inattentive to fear (as a rash person). Virtue, Aristotle argues, is like aiming for the center of a target. You can look at the extremes to aim between them (*EN* II.9). There are, after all, many more ways of going wrong than right, and the wrong ways can guide us, through process of elimination, to the right ways. The imprecision does not deter Aristotle (or me) from talking about ethics. Rather, it makes him attend to the many ways people live worse and better lives, and he distinguishes the alternatives for forming our characters. This is why I use examples and general descriptions of play and playfulness throughout. I hope that these rough strategies for characterization are good enough to give action-guiding, ethical advice—ways of evaluating the goodness of doing certain things and being certain ways. So, I cannot give precise definitions or exact semantic boundaries, but general descriptions and examples should work well enough for my purpose.

Aristotle has a dialectical method in ethics, starting with the opinions of others to lay out extant theories and then scrutinizing the ideas to see which of the alternatives holds up best.[5] I borrow this sometimes, but I will not hesitate to part with conventional understandings of "playfulness." Aristotle may have liked common sense more than I do. In fact, my readers would be well served by avoiding strict associations of "playfulness" with general frivolity, whimsicality, mischievousness, or participating in games. My definition of "playfulness" will differ substantially from some colloquial uses. However, the payoff of my occasional departures from extant opinions is that my characterization will be able to explain the most important associations, and it will distinguish between genuine, good types of play and false, bad types. That is, while I begin with conventional ideas and take on the mess of human ethical life, I also want structure and discrimination where possible, even if that means forging a new path through the debate. I think Aristotle sometimes does something similar. For example, in *Nicomachean Ethics*, he separates the real, virtuous courage from other 'courages,' like the 'courage' of people who overcome fear-inducing situations because they fear public shame, or like the 'courage' that some soldiers exhibit because they fear what their officers will do to them if they disobey. These mimic courage, but Aristotle argues they are not it. Analogously, there are many things that people call "playful" that I exclude from proper playfulness.

My Hypotheses and Vocabulary

Long in short: I argue that playful people use their leisure time well, and all happy people are playful. I argue so in Chapter 4, but it takes me three other chapters to set this up.

The many puzzles about play are what lead me back to Aristotle. I hope that by tracing the concept back to Aristotle, I can find a useful starting point for our conversation. Chapter 1 reviews Aristotle's take on play, the action. Aristotle has a mixed opinion of play. In some ways, it is necessary for human life, as when it helps children to develop or adults to rest their bodies and minds after stress and labor. Yet, Aristotle also argues that play is insufficient for a good life, and he derides it venomously when it encourages loose morals. Chapter 1 establishes the ways play gets evaluated ethically by Aristotle. It is central to my conception of playfulness because it associates play with leisure, and it shows leisure to be something that we must use well in order to live good lives.

Chapter 2, then, builds on Chapter 1's insight that play has ethical stakes. It summarizes the core concepts of Aristotelian ethical theory to evaluate play. Here, I summarize primarily the values of happiness (*eudaimonia*) and virtue (*aretē*), and I show why leisure (*scholē*) is so important for Aristotle.

Many words are difficult to translate, so let me mark some curiosities here. I translate *eudaimonia* in various ways. Most commonly, I render it as "happiness" because it is a common word today, and people still consider the pursuit of happiness worthwhile. But sometimes I choose "flourishing," which emphasizes that *eudaimonia* takes time and commitment to achieve, and it is something that actualizes a potential in human life becoming the best it can. "Flourishing" separates Aristotle's actual use of *eudaimonia* from contemporary tendencies to view "happiness" as an acute, emotional state. No doubt, flourishing entails positive emotions and moods, but it cannot be reduced to them; it is more an accomplishment of a person cultivating her whole self and living her entire life well. "Happiness" and "flourishing" will be synonymous for me, and I switch between them to emphasize different aspects of *eudaimonia*.

Similarly, I render *aretē* (plural: *aretai*) in various ways. Most often, I render it as "virtue" since this word captures the positivity of developing a good character. Sometimes, I choose "excellence" because it emphasizes the activity of forming good character, in that a human must perform tasks well and over time to develop *aretai*. Virtues take work to develop, and they almost always benefit their possessors' lives. Or, so Aristotle argues (and I assume). "Virtue" and "excellence" are synonymous, but (again) they emphasize different aspects.

Relatedly, sometimes, I discuss "moral character traits," which technically apply to both *aretai* (virtues) and *kakai* (vices). There is a sprawling contemporary literature on virtues, vices, and their psychological characteristics.[6] But unfortunately, I do not have space to summarize it. Generally speaking, though, moral character traits are deeply engrained ways of acting, thinking, and feeling, much like habits (but bigger and more complicated). They are "moral" because they impact our lives in moral ways. They do this by inclining us to flounder or flourish when facing unavoidable, universal situations in human life. For example, all humans face fear—from reacting to things that go bump in the night to reacting to the things that go bump in our capitalist hellscape that threaten to disintegrate every aspect of who we are and how we love one another. Yet, if you do not learn to face fear well, it creates moral problems. By contrast, if you develop the trait of courage, you will face any fear-eliciting circumstance well, no matter the domain of life, no matter whether the fear is elicited by asking a romantic interest to dinner, negotiating a raise from your boss, or facing a terminal illness. All the ways that we face fear train us to become courageous or cowardly or some other predictable pattern of character. As you probably sense, this gets complicated. I avoid many complications by focusing on offering a way to organize observations about playfulness specifically. I am committed to the theory that playfulness is a global, moral character trait. But, even if it is something else (perhaps a local, aesthetic trait), my analysis should be useful. Few people have addressed playfulness in any respect, so I hope that, if I am wrong, my errors provide a productive foil.

A last note on my language: I use "ethical" and "moral" synonymously, but I more strictly mean "ethical." In ancient Greek, *ēthos* refers to customs, character, and habits. It deals with wide-scope aspects of character traits and flourishing and how people judge and interact with each other. I mean "ethical" because part of being a neo-Aristotelian virtue ethicist (which I have already confessed to) is refusing any evaluation of a person's actions without contextualized information about a person's character, life narrative, and particular socio-historical circumstances involving interactions with specific institutions. I cannot accurately evaluate someone's action without knowing who she is and what situation she is in. Ethical obligations address what a person should do to develop herself virtuously and achieve happiness given her particularities. By contrast, "moral" usually has a more focused scope on principles, values, or individual actions, often apart from individual particularities, sometimes without reference to human experience at all. I almost always speak of the moral in terms of the ethical. Chapter 2 lays out the basic components of the concepts noted here. But it does not defend them, as each would require a book-length treatment.

Chapter 3 lays the last piece of the foundation by addressing the topic of play and the many ways people discuss it. But instead of addressing the works of other philosophers, Chapter 3 builds on the life and social sciences. This chapter makes the point that play helps individual organisms to develop psychological skills to cope with stress and learn about the world. In social animals, it also helps organisms to bond with each other and communicate optimal ways of performing different actions. Yet, while these points apply to humans, humans are more complicated, so we must contextualize the research about non-humans. This is because humans use values in play. It happens in the games of children, who imitate social

6 *Introduction*

roles, and it happens in the playful actions of adults in spaces like cafes and taverns, where people can come together during leisure time to exchange ideas and culture. Humans, especially, use reason and complex sociality to play, and there is no non-human analogue. Human play shares some characteristics with non-humans, but it seems inextricable from ethical and political values. Chapter 3 thus surveys some empirical work to talk about play's many dimensions.

Chapter 4 is the most important chapter of the work, as it sets out my theory of playfulness. The critical and curious alike will want to focus there. In neo-Aristotelian fashion, I tie the virtue of playfulness to a sphere of life: leisure. By "leisure," I almost always mean leisure time, the time that we have that serves no direct somatic, economic, or otherwise necessary goal; the time that we have to be free and choose what we do for its own sake. And I argue that *playfulness helps us to use our leisure time to rest, develop ourselves, and engage our communities*. I also argue that playful people must be serious, creative, humble, optimistic, and social. They should also avoid being flaky, severe, rigid, unruly, fragile, reckless, and unjust. This theory hopefully shows the ways that playful people use their leisure time to improve themselves and pursue happiness. Playfulness involves the various facets of an Aristotelian virtue—right thoughts, emotions, and motivations; and right actions, manners of execution, and aspects of social awareness.

Some critics might be concerned that my theory of playfulness makes too much of playfulness or renders certain things playful that should not be. I think a playful person, for example, can express playfulness when resting, being idle, playing a game, or relating with others. Whatever they use their leisure time for, playful people are playful when they use it well. Critics might take my theory of playfulness as too broad. However, I hope that my theory identifies the sphere of life that playfulness interacts with and gives a way of distinguishing between good and bad uses of leisure time. I hope that it explains the jumbled data on play by contextualizing playful actions in the life of a playful person. Other critics will worry that my characterization of playfulness ignores malicious things in play. But here, again, I appeal to Aristotle. Playfulness, by definition, is ethical. But there are unethical aspects of improper playfulness, which I try to explain. The ultimate conclusion of this chapter is: *playfulness is a necessary condition for flourishing; happy people are playful people*. And the ultimate conclusion of the book is that happy people play, and playful people live. We become most who we are in our leisure time, and playfulness ensures that who we are is excellent.

Playfulness as Serious Business

Play and playfulness involve much more than games or sports. Ancient Athens proves this too. Politicians used festivals, spectacles, and athletic contests to win favor from citizens and non-citizens, and they used the luxurious prizes paid to competitors as ways of publicizing their wealth. Olympian victors in the most popular events won $700,000 for first place, and Panathenaic winners received $130,000 worth of olive oil. This extravagance was not despised by the lower classes either; they identified with the diligence and endurance of the athletes, reminding laborers of their crafts or citizens of their times rowing warships. Sometimes, these athletes used their fortunes and reputations to enter politics, and sometimes, they were executed or ostracized for opposing tyrants, as with Kallias, son of Didymias. What gets lost in many histories, though, is that many of the athletic festivals (e.g., the Panathenaic ones) included religious processions, public performances of theater and music, and closing ceremonies that used animal sacrifices for large feasts. In the rituals of play, the ethical and political mixed, and the soul was never neglected for the body. In fact, philosophy's most prestigious schools—Plato's Academy and Aristotle's Lyceum—were gymnasiums built for training athletes and citizens long before they housed the lectures of philosophers.[7] This plethora of activities hints at one important thing: leisure time impacts life profoundly, and there are many ways of using it. I hope that this book makes us protect our leisure time and use it well.

Playfulness, for me, is the way of sorting the good from the bad in such a diverse sphere of life as leisure. Why, then, do we not talk about play more often? And more pertinently, why do we not care about leisure and playfulness—who plays, how they play, and what makes some types of play ethical or just? I will not offer any psychological explanations for the neglect of these questions in philosophy, but I will offer an experimental treatment in this book.

To see the contemporary relevance of my questions and the ways the Athenians are similar to us, one need only consider millionaire athletes and their philanthropy, like LeBron James and his I Promise School, which gives its students free bicycles, meals, and college tuition after they graduate. Or consider National Basketball Association athletes who protested China's treatment of Hong Kong in 2019, or ex-National Football League quarterback Colin Kaepernick who started the trend of kneeling during the American National Anthem to protest police brutality against Black people in America, beginning in 2016 and continuing today. Or, we can consider the high incidences of chronic traumatic encephalopathy (CTE) among National Football League players or their violent offense records. Or, we can examine athletes-turned-politicians like Dwight Eisenhower and Arnold Schwarzenegger. These examples show how play affects our abilities to live well and to reflect on what our communities value; it affects who we are and how who we are has political implications. Or, as Ursula K. Le Guin once wrote, "How you play is what you win."[8] Play affects our lives, and it does not seem to be ethically or politically neutral. So, we need a way of assessing it. I hope to offer one method by arguing that play affects our characters and that a good life requires playfulness.

Notes

1 Diogenes Laertius, *Lives of Eminent Philosophers*, trans. Pamela Mensch (Oxford: Oxford University Press, 2018), III.4, p. 135. For disagreement on Plato's name, see: James A. Notopoulos, "The Name of Plato," *Classical Philology*, vol. 34, no. 2 (Apr. 1939): pp. 135–45. It is funny that Plato, the wrestler, was never tried for crimes against the State, nor did Athens try to execute him. But his chatty teacher, Socrates, and his aristocratic student, Aristotle, were.
2 See: Philippa Foot, *Virtues and Vices* (Oxford: Oxford University Press, 2002); Rosalind Hursthouse, *On Virtue Ethics* (Oxford: Oxford University Press, 1999); and Martha Nussbaum, *The Fragility of Goodness: Luck and Ethics in Greek Tragedy and Philosophy*, Updated Ed. (Cambridge: Cambridge University Press, 2001). For the history and influence of some of these women, see: Benjamin J. B. Lipscomb, *The Women Are Up to Something: How Elizabeth Anscombe, Philippa Foot, Mary Midgley, and Iris Murdoch Revolutionized Ethics* (Oxford: Oxford University Press, 2022); Clare MacCumhaill and Rachael Wiseman, *Metaphysical Animals: How Four Women Brought Philosophy Back to Life* (New York: Doubleday, 2022).
3 Marcus Aurelius, *Meditations*, trans. Gregory Hays (New York: Modern Library, 2003), VI.21.
4 Notable exceptions are Maria Lugones, Emily Ryall, Lukáš Mareš, and Michael Ridge (as well as respondents such as Mariana Ortega and Ricardo Friaz), who all analyze playfulness.
5 For more on Aristotle's dialectic, see: D. W. Hamlyn, "Aristotle on Dialectic," *Philosophy*, vol. 65, no. 254 (Oct. 1990): pp. 465–76.
6 For extended contemporary treatments of character, see: Christian Miller, *Character and Moral Psychology* (Oxford: Oxford University Press, 2014); Mark Alfano, *Character as Moral Fiction* (Cambridge: Cambridge University Press, 2013); and John Doris, *Lack of Character: Personality and Moral Behavior* (Cambridge: Cambridge University Press, 2002).
7 Donald G. Kyle, *Sport and Spectacle in the Ancient World*, 2nd ed. (West Sussex: Wiley Blackwell, 2015), esp. chs. 8 and 10. The Pythian Games deserve mention too. In tribute to Apollo (both an archer and artist himself), they included competitions for songs, instrumental music, acting, dancing, and painting. I owe Scott F. Aikin for this reference.
8 Ursula K. Le Guin, "The Matter of Seggri," in: *The Birthday of the World and Other Stories* (New York: Perennial, 2002), p. 59.

1 Aristotle on Play as Medicine

Before Aristotle: Heraclitus the Champion of Play and Plato the Critic

As is typical, philosophers do not agree on much. Their opinions on play follow this trend. Even in ancient Greece, where philosophy had yet to mature, two camps already quibbled before Aristotle wrote a thing. One is best represented by Heraclitus. He wrote, "Life is a child playing, gaming; the ruling power is a child's."[1] Like most of Heraclitus' writing, the quote is cryptic. We can only speculate about what he means, since only fragments of his work survive, and we know little definitive about the games he would have known. But a good guess is that Heraclitus meant that play enraptures the player, and its pretenses are harmless, or at least agreed upon by the players at the outset of the game. There is a purity to children playing, children who experience happiness directly and have no need of asking for happiness' definition or its interactions with external affairs. Children playing represent the most important parts of life—flourishing and creating. And these capacities have no need of intellect, reputation, luxury, or even detailed explanation. In Heraclitus' philosophy, play is elevated from a meaningless trifle for children to life itself. It is the key to understanding the deep nature of reality.

Plato represents the other camp. His view is most famously expressed in *Republic*.[2] There, Plato proposes an educational model that uses music and art to educate people on proper morals. For him, music can directly move the soul, and narratives make us sympathize with the characters and their lives. Plato argues that educators in the *kallipolis*, the beautiful city, should harness play's power to form good citizens. Play is a formidable pedagogical tool, and it can help make us into good people. However, not all art is edifying, and especially not the most popular works by poets such as Homer or tragedians such as Sophocles. As a direct result of its pedagogical power, Plato censors art. Both immoral art and the artists who make it are condemned and expelled from the

10 *Aristotle on Play as Medicine*

kallipolis. Plato worries that many artists misrepresent their subjects and that the inaccuracies in artworks corrupt audiences. For example, artists fail to even get the simple things right. If you have ever been on a theater or film set, you have seen how the rooms are made of façades and the props are not functional. For Plato, it is clear that artists satisfy only appearances, not practical uses or higher ideals. But the audience *thinks* that the sets and props are real and that the interactions between characters are believable, at least if the art is effective. The audience, therefore, falls in love with lies. Worse, according to Plato, artists depict the gods and heroes of Greek religion as vicious, thus not only misrepresenting mundane objects and affairs but also the very ideals embedded in communities. The gods and heroes are supposed to be people we admire and model our lives after; they take center stage in productions and our moral imaginations. And this means that when artists portray them as monsters, the effects are worth alarm. For example, Zeus rapes many women in many ways—Leda as a swan, Danae as golden rain, Europa as a bull, and his own mother, Rhea, as a snake.[3] Additionally, arguably one of the best people in Greek poetry, Priam, King of Troy, is beaten to death by his infant grandson (the infant being the son of Hector, Priam's good son, who was killed and defiled by Achilles).[4] The depravity is inventive and inextricable from Greek theater and poetry. Moreover, these stories are not one-off tales; they are integral parts of the epics that gave Greeks their identities, and these gruesome tidbits are representative of entire genres such as tragedy. Many plays center on horror, such as the tragedies of Euripides. In *Hekabe*, for example, the titular Queen of Troy is taken prisoner after the Greeks sack her city. She watches as her innocent daughter is sacrificed to sate the ghost of Achilles, and she finds her young son's body washed up on the shore, clearly having been murdered by people who were supposed to shelter him. So, she takes her revenge. She convinces the man who murdered her son to come into a tent, and her handmaids murder his children in front of him, and then she gouges out his eyes. The last thing he sees in his sighted life is the murder of his children.[5] Plato worries that such art might give us the wrong impression. It might whet, not quell, our appetites for lust, revenge, and impulse. And that spells doom for large groups of people who are even *slightly* influenced by such depraved art. After all, it is not OK to commit even the slightest bit of murder like Hekabe.

Philosophers might want more nuance in the previous views. But that is unnecessary for the takeaway lesson here: play—part of what we do in our leisure—is valued in radically different ways. On the one hand, the Heraclitean aspect assesses play positively. On the other, the Platonic views it with suspicion. And this forms the context for Aristotle's remarks.

Aristotle tries to make sense of the conflicting accounts on play. And in this chapter, I argue that he tries to mediate the disagreements by relating play to many ethical concepts. By relating play to relaxation and childhood development, Aristotle defends the Heraclitean view that it is inextricable from human life and should be preserved. But by relating play to flourishing, pleasure, and leisure, Aristotle defends the Platonic view that play ought to be assessed with moral scrutiny.

Aristotle, therefore, holds a deep ambivalence about play. He sees it as a *pharmakon*, the Greek word for "drug" that can be rendered equally as "medicine" or "poison."[6] And like any medicine, play begs careful study to get the dosage right.

Before continuing, I must note two difficulties in addressing this topic. First, play is mixed in its evaluations by Aristotle, so sometimes I must address the positive to get to the negative, or the negative in the positive. However, I have attempted to minimize any back-and-forth to make your job easier as a reader. Second, even though I argue that Aristotle organizes the extant views on play in Greece and that they form a coherent position, I must admit that his remarks are scattered throughout his works and difficult to piece together. In my opinion, the biggest challenge is a linguistic problem. It is difficult to render accurately into English the Greek words related to play. *Paidiē* is the most direct word for play, but it also gets translated as "childish play," "sport," "game," "pastime," and sometimes "amusement."[7] The verb for play, *paizō*, has similarly broad associations, such as "play," "jest," and "invent in a playful spirit." Adding complications, *paidiē* and *paizō* share the root *pais*, which relates to the Greek word *pais*, "child," and more loosely *paideia*, "education" (but most literally concerns the upbringing of children). The Greek root *pais*, therefore, connects the concepts of play, playfulness, child, childishness, sport, game, amusement, and education. And translators face a difficult task of maintaining distinctions between concepts while showing their tight relationship. I try to pull insights from all relevant topics to assemble my interpretation of Aristotle's thoughts on play, and I bracket the Greek text where relevant.[8]

If you only take one thing away from this chapter, it should be that the most important idea in Aristotle's remarks on play is that he connects it to leisure. Leisure, for Aristotle, is the time we have away from work or any type of necessity. *Scholē*, the Greek word for leisure, is the opposite of *ascholia*, the word for work or business, literally "non-leisure."[9] Leisure time is essential for living a good life, and the justice of communities can be measured by how much leisure its citizens have and what they do with that time. This connection between play and leisure will be crucial for the later chapters.

The Heraclitean Aspect in Aristotle's Theory: Play as Medicine

One of the most unique things in Aristotle's remarks about play is that he calls it a medicine, *pharmakon*. He argues that it can help tired and stressed people to relax. And anyone who has been alive the past few years, or really at all, knows the importance of that. Aristotle goes as far as to say that relaxation and play are necessities in life (*EN* 1128b3-4). Aristotle explains:

> Play [*paidiais*] is needed more amid serious occupations [*ascholiais*] than at other times (for he who is hard at work [*ponōn*] has need of relaxation [*anapauseōs*], and play [*paidia*] gives relaxation, whereas occupation is always accompanied with exertion and effort). We should introduce amusements [*paidias*] only at suitable times, and they should be our medicines [*pharmakeias*], for the emotion which they create in the soul is relaxation [*anesis*] and from the pleasure we obtain rest [*anapausis*].
>
> (*Pol.* 1337b37-1338a1)

This excerpt argues that people who work hard or attend to serious matters are most in need of play because play offers relaxation, rest, and pleasure. Play is literally medicine that stops the ache of the day-to-day grind.[10] And it is a medicine that can relax and rest the entire person, both body and mind. Play's main therapeutic effect is generated by the emotions of rest and relaxation and the sensation of pleasure. These effects happen both during and after play. It is important to emphasize that play is not merely for brutes to help them rest their bodies. Rather, there is an acute and potent psychological effect as well. Adult life is difficult on our bodies and minds. And play heals both.

Aristotle observes that most flourishing people enjoy their pastimes and take refuge in them (*EN* 1176b12-13). Consider, for example, how friends who get together often play games, tell jokes, and reminisce about good times. They not only talk about harrowing struggles and heroic victories. They also prize the small, light moments. I played football in Texas when I was in high school. And some of my favorite memories are not about the games we won, and they certainly are not about the sweltering August practices. They are about the jokes and pranks in the locker room after practice or games, when we were too exhausted to do much else. And today, these are the stories that I tell most when talking about those days with my former teammates or others. Aristotle knew that there was something to the downtime, the in-between time, the moments that many philosophers are tempted to overlook. But looking back, we often find that those small moments of respite meant more than we thought they did at the time.

The rest, relaxation, and amusement that we take in other people is so important that Aristotle dedicates an entire virtue to it: wit, *eutrapelia*. This social play of amusing ourselves and friends, and simply enjoying each other's company, is ubiquitous and necessary for a good life. However, Aristotle argues that social amusements can be done in better or worse ways. Buffoons, for example, take every opportunity to make jokes and be vulgar. Stiffs stray in the opposite direction, neither making nor taking jokes, nor relishing the pleasures of social amusements.[11] But the witty few, they have a proper appreciation for social pleasures, and they develop a sense of wit that enables them to cultivate pleasant interactions with others in their downtime. Consider the conversation of coworkers resting before they get back to work. Aristotle thinks it important to analyze the ethical dimensions of our downtime and the ways we play during it (*EN* IV.8).

Part of what makes this conversation complicated, however, is that Aristotle breaks human life into many developmental stages. His remarks on wit and relaxation show it important for adults. But he also has much to say about children. Aristotle emphasizes play's importance in childhood development. He implores parents, caretakers, and politicians to preserve play in the lives of children. He argues that children under the age of five need to avoid both labor and study and that they instead should fill their time with play. He also warns that people should never stop children who cry and scream because both behaviors are crucial to their proper development (*Pol.* VII.17). In these remarks, he not only describes play's role in childhood development like a psychologist would, but he also argues for ethical and political protections of that play.

In fact, his major political treatise, *Politics*, ends with an educational program for children and adolescents that includes play. He is direct in his rationale, "No one will doubt that the legislator should direct his attention above all to the education of youth; for the neglect of education does harm to the constitution" (*Pol.* 1337a10-11). In other words, Aristotle argues that the only way to maintain a just, healthy, or strong state is to ensure that the youth are educated well. Aristotle breaks with certain Greek traditions, so he has to make a case for his general system. For example, rather than continue in the Greek tradition of private tutors or family-based education, Aristotle argued that education in the most important subjects should be accessible to everyone (1337b22-4). Just states require as many educated people as possible. You protect a state by educating good citizens. To do this, Aristotle proposes a quadrivium, four subjects that education in just societies must cover: *gramma* (reading and writing), *gymnasion* (physical training), *graphē* (drawing), and *mousikē* (music and poetry). What interests me about this quadrivium is that it not only includes practical things, such as reading, writing, and drawing (here meant in the sense of diagraming or drafting). Such things are useful for communication and conducting business. Literate, articulate people do business well. Aristotle guessed no one would disagree with *gramma* and *graphē* for that reason. These disciplines make the state money. *Gymnasion* is not as practical, however. And he knew that he had to defend this idea. After all, wrestling, running, and playing games might be seen as superfluous by some. Aristotle did not think to mention the positive effects of

14 Aristotle on Play as Medicine

gymnasion on the health of the body. But he did mention how it cultivates courage, *andreia*. This is coded language in the Greco-Roman world. *Andreia* means courage but can also be translated as "manliness." *Andreia* shares the root of *anēr*, which means man, specifically gendered masculine. (Similarly, the Latin *virtus* means courage, and *vir* means man.) I think he knew that opponents of his educational system would retract their criticisms of *gymnasion* if they heard manliness was at stake. So, the games and sports that would naturally happen in *gymnasion* gain their public support from macho Greeks in a rhetorical appeal to masculinity. That leaves the last of the quadrivium, *mousikē*, to justify. And this one is the trickiest.

Mousikē, in many languages, looks like the word related to music, and it is in Greek too. But in Greek, it also relates to *Mousai*, the Muses. *Musikē* literally involves the artforms that the Muses preside over. And in ancient Greece, that was most directly experienced in narrative poetry set to music, especially as read in public and performed on stages at rituals and festivals. Think of Hesiod, Homer, Aristophanes, Sophocles, etc. So, Aristotle is arguing for a public education (as opposed to private) that includes reading, writing, and drawing (fine, that is good for business), and sport (OK, that makes people manly) and music.

A critic might ask incredulously, so now you want to set up an educational system to turn all the children into musical theater majors? I must admit that I am imagining an alarmist opponent to Aristotle because no such one exists in the text. But Athens exiled Aristotle at the end of his life, so I do not think that I am far off. And the fact that later historians preserved Aristotle's image as thin-calved, beady-eyed, and luxuriously clothed, it is easy to imagine hypermasculine Greeks reacting to his words in this way.[12] In any event, imagine your own child telling you that he wants to study wrestling and poetry (especially compared to your other child telling you that she wants to study math or drafting). Aristotle knew that he had to say something to defend this part of the quadrivium.

First, he defends leisure (*scholē*), the free time that we have away from direct necessities and that we can use to pursue such things as sport and music. He says,

> Nature herself, as has been often said, requires that we should be able, not only to work well [*ascholein orthōs*] but to use leisure well [*scholazein dunasthai kalōs*]; for, as I must repeat once again, the first principle of all action is leisure.
>
> (*Pol.* 1337b30-33)

In other words, we work hard and do difficult things so that we can protect and enjoy our leisure time. And if we lacked leisure time, our lives would lack something important.

Aristotle on Play as Medicine 15

But why should Aristotle argue so strongly for the importance of leisure? He offers a few reasons. First, for him, leisure itself is necessary for enjoying life and cultivating happiness, and those without leisure have trouble doing either (*Pol.* 1338a1-4). Aristotle writes, "To be always seeking after the useful [*chrēsimon*] does not become free [*eleutheriois*] and exalted souls [*megalopsuchois*]" (*Pol.* 1338b2-4). Human life is about more than mere utility or connecting every action to a direct purpose. The best kinds of people do more than work; they take time to enjoy life and cultivate aspects of their personality unrelated to survival. And the best kinds of people value their companions beyond their professional or social usefulness; they make time to enjoy each other's company or improve their lives together. Not only does spending leisure well cultivate mental and social health, but it also creates cooperative and engaged citizens. This is why Aristotle turns his attention to leisure in *Politics*.

Second, and one of the boldest defenses of leisure, is through a rebuke of Athens' biggest political rival, Sparta. He diagnoses Sparta's failure as a state as not being able to live in times of peace and leisure (*Pol.* VII.14). Yes, Sparta could wage war. But in times of peace, their iron lost its edge. They fell apart. Aristotle is vehemently anti-imperialist. For him, it is unsustainable. It makes no sense to go to war or fight for resources without strong reasons. War for war's sake is ridiculous to him. So, reflecting on why we go to war and why we work hard, Aristotle repeats something that becomes a motto: people should only go to war for the sake of peace, and they should only work for the sake of leisure (repeated three times, *Pol.* 1271b5-6, 1333a35-6, 1334a13-15). In other words, what good is war if there is no peace to enjoy afterward, and what good is labor if there is no enjoying the leisure that follows? But there is a catch. The only way to learn to enjoy peace and leisure is through education. Aristotle advocates for a liberal arts education because he wants people to be free. "Liberal" here literally means "free." The reason Aristotle thinks that everyone should be educated in reading, writing, drawing, physical education, and art is that it teaches you to use your free time well. In those circumstances where you do not need to do anything, you reveal what you most value. And the Spartans could only start another war because that is all they knew. Aristotle pulls no punches here. He says, "And for this the legislator is to blame, he never having taught them how to lead the life of leisure [*dunasthai scholazein*]" (*Pol.* 1334a9-10).[13] Forever wars only work in science fiction cultures, as in Star Trek's Klingons or Warhammer 40,000's many factions. In real life, forever wars kill people, cultures, and the freest parts of ourselves. But art and play preserve and promote life, humanity, and freedom. This is why everyone in a just community would be educated not only in practical things but also in beautiful things, things that serve no further purpose than the thing or experience itself. People must be taught to handle their freedom; otherwise, they start more wars like

Sparta, or they engage in more consumption that eventually starts more wars. Peace and leisure are vital to justice. Aristotle argues that peace and leisure ought to be the goals of all military measures (*Pol.* 1334a3-5) and that the goodness of citizens, rulers, and states can be partially measured by how much leisure time they have and what they do with that time (*Pol.* II.9, 11; IV.6; VII.5, 9). Good states allow as many of their people to flourish as possible, and their rulers and citizens need leisure to cultivate intellectual capacities to help them organize and rule society more justly. Leisure is at the root of justice, philosophy, and happiness.

In Aristotle, we see a historic shift for Greece. Leisure did not always exist in human history, nor was it always valued. In Archaic Greece (roughly the three centuries before Socrates), Greeks saw work itself as sacred. You can see this reflected in the works of Hesiod. He called his Archaic contemporaries a "race of iron" who "will never cease from toil and misery by day or night."[14] And he proclaimed, "It is from work that men are rich in flocks and wealthy, and a working man is much dearer to the immortals. Work is no reproach, but not working is a reproach."[15] However, things changed. By Classical Greece (the period of Socrates, Plato, and Aristotle), people generally began to value leisure, not only in philosophy, but also in popular plays and poems. Classical Greeks started contrasting leisure (*scholē*) with labors (*ponoi*), mobs (*ochloi*), riches (*ploutos*), and even the busyness of political rivalries. Moreover, Greeks started to associate leisure with rest (*anapausis*) and happiness (*eudaimonia*).[16] Aristotle's arguments make it explicit: the goal of an individual person's life and of a state is the same, leisure and peace (*Pol.* 1134a10-15). Or, in his own words,

> ...it is peculiarly disgraceful not to be able to use them [the goods of life] in time of leisure—to show excellent qualities in action and war, and when they have peace and leisure to be no better than slaves.
> (1334a35-9)

If you want to be a free person, you have to be able to use your leisure time well.

The challenge of combining these comments is to figure out why play seems to pop up in the lives of happy people so often. And for that, I think the key is that Aristotle usually relates play to leisure, which becomes a pillar concept for his philosophy. For Aristotle, leisure (*scholē*) is necessary for a full, flourishing human life (*EN* 1177b4-5).[17] Without leisure, people cannot develop capacities for reflection, creativity, or political involvement. And without these capacities and activities, people cannot be considered truly happy. Aristotle repeats throughout *Politics* that, while humans must work to secure goods necessary for living (e.g., food, shelter, and social coordination), leisure is better than toil, and leisure is the goal of all labor (*Pol.* VII.3, 1334a14-20, 1333b1-2). He argues this most poignantly when claiming that leisure is the first principle of all action, as we saw above (*Pol.* 1337b31-33).

It matters for play that leisure is important for life. Simply put, we need leisure to live well, and play is a pleasurable part of that leisure. This, then, implies that at least *part* of our leisure—the very goal and product of our professional labor and political organization—should be spent in play. The best human lives include leisure, and play is part of that. The best human lives include pleasure, and play generates that. Therefore, for Aristotle, play will be found in every flourishing human life—in the amusement of children, the relaxation of adults, the pontificating of philosophers, and the social cohesion of communities.

You are probably getting the sense of the difficulty here. Aristotle thinks that adults should use their downtime to amuse themselves and rest, but not so much that they become buffoons. He thinks children should be allowed to run and scream and play, but only until they are five years old. Readers of Aristotle will get the sense that play is important, but they will be left with the question: how important? And here, I can offer two interpretative options. First, we could hold a weak, *coinstantiation view* about play and happiness. This view says that play and happiness are merely coinstantiated, or things that appear together for whatever reason. This weak interpretation would make no further commitments with respect to how or why. It would only mark that happy people tend also to be people who play at some time. Young people play. Adults play. And happy people, having lived through childhood and adulthood, obviously play too. But who knows why? Contrastingly, a second and stronger option would be a *causal view*. Other interpreters of Aristotle might say that he is making a *causal* claim about the relationship between play and happiness, where one *affects* the other, such as happiness producing play or *vice versa*. Here, the idea is that there is a deeper connection between play on the one hand and happiness on the other, and this connection goes beyond mere coincidental coinstantiation. There is a causal explanation for why they appear together. Aristotle himself does little to argue for how strict the relationship between play and happiness is. The only things that are clear in this metaphysical sense are that (a) play and happiness are not identical and are distinct things, and (b) play is often (maybe always) included in the lives of happy people.

At minimum, Aristotle's remarks on play in *Nicomachean Ethics* and *Politics* show that play is a natural part of life. For children, it facilitates development. For adults, it aids in rest, and it is cherished when reflecting on life with others. At whatever stage in human life, people should value play, and Aristotle affords it an important place in life that should not be eliminated altogether. Ridding people of play would detrimentally affect childhood development and adults' abilities to rest and relax. Heraclitus died over a century before Aristotle was born. But had Heraclitus and Aristotle lived at the same time, they could have agreed that play is crucial for life.

The Platonic Aspect in Aristotle's Theory: Play as Poison

Despite the positive qualities that Aristotle ascribed to play, and despite his defense of *mousikē* as essential for education, he also had significant reservations. It is easiest to let him speak for himself:

> Indeed, there is nothing which the legislator should be more careful to drive away than indecency of speech; for the light utterance [*eucherōs legein*] of shameful words leads soon to shameful actions. The young especially should never be allowed to repeat or hear anything of the sort. A freemen who is found saying or doing what is forbidden, if he be too young as yet to have the privilege of reclining at the public tables, should be disgraced and beaten ... And since we do not allow improper language, clearly we should also banish pictures or speeches from the stage which are indecent. ... the legislator should not allow youth to be spectators of iambi or of comedy until they are of an age to sit at the public tables and to drink strong wine; by that time education [*paideia*] will have armed them against the evil influences of such representations.
>
> (*Pol.* 1336b4-23)

Here, Aristotle sounds a lot like Plato banning the poets from the *kallipolis*.[18] He explicitly worries that careless talk about shameful things makes those shameful things easier to do. Aristotle claims that stories prepare the youth for life and set expectations, so immoral art trains them incorrectly. It is important to remember that Greek comedy is different from the reverent attitude many Americans have toward ancient Greece. People might read, if anyone, Plato and Aristotle, or maybe Homer and Sophocles. But most do not read Aristophanes or about Dionysus. This means we forget that Aristophanes repeatedly makes fart jokes in *Clouds*, and the plot of his *Lysistrata* is that women are trying to end the Peloponnesian War by withholding sex from their husbands. Also, cults of Dionysus were strong in Greece. Artwork depicted him and related characters like Priapus with huge, red erections, and there were often parades where worshippers adorned and carried around penises. This helps make sense of Aristotle's remarks about obscenity. Aristotle observes that we favor what we first come to know. So, we should keep kids away from badness, vice, and hate so that they avoid bias in favor of these qualities (*Pol.* VII.17).[19] The positive sensations associated with play should not be associated with unsavory things. There is truth behind every joke, and immoral jokes are no exception. For example, consider how Bill Cosby joked about drugging women before it came out that he actually was, or how Louis C. K. frequently joked about masturbating before he harassed women in that way.[20] However, Aristotle does not think people powerless to irreverent art (unlike his teacher Plato). He expresses confidence in education, or youth that have been taught well to withstand the temptations of vice. Rather than banning things outright like Plato, Aristotle censors them for children below the drinking age because by then their education will have done its job. This introduces a critical complication to Aristotle's thoughts on play. Play is not all good, as Heraclitus implies, even if Aristotle protects it for children and adults and builds it into education. Rather, play also has a darker side. Aristotle shows the influence that his teacher Plato had on him by placing many constraints on play (especially for children).

As covered in the previous section, Aristotle observes that play produces pleasure. But he has two interesting explanations for why. First, it lacks compulsion: "Hence ease [*rathymiai*], freedom from toil [*aponiai*], relaxation [*ameleiai*], play [*paidiai*], rest [*anapauseis*], and sleep belong to the class of pleasant things; for these are all free from any element of compulsion [*anagkēn*]" (*Rhet.* 1370a12-15).[21] Because play lacks forcible demands, it feels pleasant to the player. Because you *do not need* to play, play feels good. Before moving on to his second reason for play's pleasantness, I need to note a host of complications in this "lack of necessity" aspect. Aristotle's remarks on play and its lack of necessity raise questions about what "necessity" means and whether introducing necessity debases the status of the activity as play, its pleasure, or both. He only says that the lack of necessity is what makes play pleasant. At least two interpretations are possible here. First, Aristotle could be making a *metaphysical* claim about the activity, where play loses its status as play or its pleasant quality if biological, economic, social, or political necessity directly bears on it. Second, he could be making an *experiential* claim about the mindset of the player, that a player cannot *feel* outside compulsion to play for it to be pleasant or to be considered play (even if such necessities exist). The obvious case here would be professional athletes or gamers. If the metaphysical reading is right, then Aristotle would say they are not playing because their biological, economic, and social livelihoods depend on the playing. Or this somehow changes the nature of the pleasure, maybe downgrading it. But if the experiential reading is right, professionals could properly play or feel full pleasure, as long as they do not feel the necessities while playing. But I think another example is probably more relatable. And that is how we evaluate rehearsal or practice for playing—the activities that you have to do to get better at the play. Both seem necessary for certain types of play, but it is not clear whether they are play themselves or whether they feel good. For example, it is easy to understand how playing

"Enter Sandman" on guitar is play or pleasant. But could you deem practicing pentatonic scales in E-minor to get better at the solos in "Enter Sandman" as play or pleasant? In this example, we have a different kind of necessity, the necessity to improve one's skills as a precondition of playing something at a certain level of competence. This is not biological, economic, or political, but part of the progress of the activity itself. Unfortunately, I have no room to address these problems here. But other philosophers have written about these issues.[22]

The second reason that Aristotle thinks play is pleasant is that play, games [*astragaliseis*], and contests (both combative [*machētikas*] and intellectual [*eristikas*]) present an opportunity for victory (*Rhet.* 1370b31-1371a8). Aristotle argues, "Victory is also pleasant, and not merely to the competitive but to everyone; the winner sees himself in the light of a champion, and everybody has a more or less keen appetite for being that" (*Rhet.* 1370b31-4). Play and sports are pleasurable because they present an opportunity to win, and everyone likes being a winner, or at least entertaining the thought. So, play's potential for victory also makes it a pleasurable experience. It is important to add that play can also involve things that do not have victors or goals. Aristotle includes silliness [*gelōs*] in the class of pleasant things too, which can be exemplified in people, words, or actions (*Rhet.* 1371b35-1372a1). Play can be associated with structured games and contests, but it can also take a more generalized form like joking. These explanations of play's mechanisms show that Aristotle thought play's pleasure important to explain.

However, play's connection to pleasure is not all good. Aristotle is suspicious of pleasure, and by extension, whatever produces it. He goes so far as to say that pleasure is the one thing that we should guard ourselves most against (*EN* 1109b7-12). After all, it is hard to find any person who is deficient in experiencing pleasures (*EN* 1107b6-7; *EE* 1234b8), but it is easy to find those who over-delight in amusement (*EN* 1128a14), even at the expense of their health and finances (*EN* 1176b9-11).

Additionally, not all pleasures are equal for Aristotle. For Aristotle, pleasure is not a mere raw sensation. Pleasure is what we experience when our capacities are used to their highest degrees of completion and fulfillment, when our capacities do what they were meant to do. This is why Aristotle argues that the *best* forms of pleasure perfect our *best* capacities, that is, our intellectual ones. Aristotle saw the pleasure of studying philosophy—using the characteristically human capacity of reason to understand profound truths—as importantly different from the pleasure of a good meal—using our animalistic appetites and gustatory faculties to savor dead flesh and plants. Both are pleasurable and important, but the intellectual ones are better than the somatic ones. He is so certain of this that he says that no adult would choose to live with a child's mental faculties, even if promised perfect satisfaction of those juvenile capacities (*EN* X).

Additionally, pleasures differ in quality based on their objects. Pleasures attached to good objects and activities are praiseworthy, but pleasures attached to bad ones are blameworthy. To illustrate this, he says that no person would do something incredibly pleasant if it involved engaging in utterly shameful activities, even if no pain resulted (*EN* X.4-5, esp. 1174a1-5). Guilty pleasures are heavy on the guilt because they are attached to bad objects. No matter how much I may enjoy ghost-hunting reality television, I cannot in good conscience compare its pleasures to the pleasures of fine cinema, such as films featuring John William Ferrell. Or at least on Aristotelian grounds. One engages adult, cultivated, human capacities; the other does not.

These remarks should prove that pleasure is a complicated thing for Aristotle. It is so complicated that he dedicates one of the core virtues of his system to pleasure: temperance, *sōphrosunē* (AKA moderation). (We also saw above that Aristotle established the virtue of wit to regulate social pleasures.) For Aristotle, temperate people virtuously regulate the pleasures that they experience as individuals, especially physical ones (e.g., eating, drinking, or having sex).[23] Humans are animals that can experience pleasure, and we need pleasures to fulfill our lives. But pleasures also present ethical challenges. People who enjoy too many pleasures are self-indulgent, and the pleasures that self-indulgent people pursue control many aspects of their lives, which wrecks them. Consider gluttons or gamblers. Also bad but in a different way, those who shun pleasure are ascetic boors. They live a life deprived of the fundamental human experiences of feeling good. Neither the ascetic nor the self-indulgent can flourish. Only temperate people stand a chance. This is because the temperate experience the right pleasures in the right ways (*EN* III.10-12).

Play and its associated pleasures will change their ethical value depending on who does them, in which situations, for whatever reasons or feelings. Play should not serve self-indulgence, buffoonery, or flattery. And the ascetic, boorish, and surly will neglect play to their own detriment. Consider a poker game between coworkers after a long shift. Someone addicted to gambling, or someone who belittles people at the table, plays viciously. Whereas someone who plays to enjoy the game and to form deeper friendships with colleagues plays virtuously. Play can help people live well, provided that they understand pleasure's role in life, feel good about appropriate pleasures, and find proper occasions for it. For example, a surgeon who plays crosswords during downtime between consultations with patients is more virtuous than a surgeon who plays by burning his initials into his patient's organs with the cauterizer.[24] The action of play is not morally neutral. Play can serve both good and bad ends, taking us closer to or further from happiness. The happy person is neither a pleasureless, ascetic boor nor an over-indulgent, wanton debauchee. Temperate people appreciate pleasant experiences, and witty people appreciate pleasant social interactions.

Humans have a capacity for pleasure that should be cultivated. And play is nested within such conversations about the goods and ills of pleasure. Aristotle was so ambivalent about play that he outright prohibits some behaviors. For example, he argued that the play should not be base or servile [*aneleutherous*], laborious or painful [*epiponous*], or undisciplined or loose [*aneimenas*] (*Pol.* 1336a29-30).[25] Such play forms bad habits that can influence later life. Building on this, recall the quote that opened this section where Aristotle harshly prohibited indecent speech and pictures (*Pol.* 1336b4-23). Casually saying and seeing shameful things leads to shameful action, so children especially should be forbidden from such vulgarities. But his argument is more than a developmental caution for adolescents. Aristotle extends the argument to adults too. According to Aristotle, even freemen or elders who transgress propriety deserve beatings, shame, and degradation (*Pol.* 1336b8-12). To emphasize: beatings and degradation. Strong words from the philosopher who defended play and *mousikē*. Play done viciously merits scorn and punishment. Play has ethical weight. It affects habits, and it is done with people you need respect and help from. Consider the ways department dynamics change when a holiday party and its games inadvertently showcase the addiction of the departmental lush, the duplicity of the departmental sycophant, or the sadism of the departmental leader. Play's connections to individual and social development mean it must be appropriate, or we risk marring our characters and our social standings.

Aristotle's starkest restriction on play is when he argues that play can never be sufficient for flourishing, as important as it may be otherwise. Play can never be enough to make you happy. One argument for this point begins with an observation: witty people are deeply valued by tyrants, who like to keep them in their company and dedicate ample time to pursuing their amusements.[26] Yet the playful despot's life is not complete, if he does not develop himself well or pursue the right goods, no matter how much he plays or how often he has playful people around him. Aristotle warns that people who are afforded ample leisure and many goods are in special need of justice, temperance, and philosophy to avoid insolence (*Pol.* 1334a26-35). These remarks indicate that the context of play in a person's moral life matters. Even if it can help us to relax and feel good, play cannot make us good enough people to actualize all of our psychological, ethical, and civic capacities, nor can it alone help us manage the competing goods of life.

Aristotle also argues that there are people who play and experience amusement but whom no one would consider happy. For example, slaves can enjoy amusements, but it cannot be said that slaves are happy (*EN* 1177a2-10). For Aristotle, they are a counterexample to the claim that, as long as people can play, they can be happy. So, while we do not need to be royalty to be happy, we also cannot be slaves and happy, no matter how much we play. Certain political arrangements destroy our flourishing, no matter subjective joy. The implication seems to be that, when it comes down to it, play is mostly subjective joy.

It is crucial to consider why we do what we do. For Aristotle, human actions need a goal or a purpose. Aristotle found absurd the people who intentionally suffer merely for the sake of amusement (*EN* 1176b29-30). Play and amusement do not seem like worthy goals of our self-discipline, personal development, and sustained labor in the face of challenges that come from our commitments to our values. He denounces play as the goal of action (or the purpose of work), calling such a view foolish [*ēlithion*] and childish [*paidikon*]. He agrees with Anacharsis who says that people play so that they can work later, not the other way around (*EN* 1176b32-3). We can play hard to work hard, but we should not work hard to play hard. These remarks imply that play is not an intrinsically good thing; rather, play serves the end of more serious efforts because it allows someone to rest to return to work later.[27] Part of the reason he thinks this is play's connection to leisure. We play when no necessities bear on us. So, he argued that if play were the primary thing that we should do with our leisure, then play would be the goal of life and all our efforts. We work hard and secure peace to what? Play? This is ludicrous to Aristotle, so he argues that we should not spend all of our leisure at play because it is not the goal of life (*Pol.* 1337b33-6). We spend all of our time and effort to gain leisure. And to Aristotle, it would be a wasted opportunity to spend that leisure time only at play. There are more important things to develop, such as intellectual, ethical, and civic capacities that help us live well or reform our communities. We can use free time to make ourselves more virtuous, social, and just, not merely to play. This section's remarks should prove that, even if Aristotle disagreed with his teacher Plato about many things, he certainly shared a deep influence. Like Plato, Aristotle set severe limits on play, art, and leisure-time activities.

Setting the Dosage of Play

Aristotle thought it important to address play in *Nicomachean Ethics*, *Politics*, *Rhetoric*, and other works. He discussed it in relation to flourishing, pleasure, and justice. Such wide-ranging and varied discussions make for a complicated view. The upshot of Aristotle's passages is that play is important for life, but it also has the potential to habituate children and adults in ways that will detract from their moral characters and accomplishments. Play affects individuals and their psychological development, and it can also change social dynamics. Play matters, but it matters equally *how*, *why*, and *when* people play. We need to play, but this need creates responsibility to play *well*. And even though a just state should protect play for children and ensure an education with physical games and art, and even though a just state should arrange as much leisure as possible for all citizens, that same state should keep children away from bad influences, and its community members should beat the most shameful players.

On the one hand, we can see the Heraclitean element. Aristotle argued that play is an ineliminable part of life because it helps children to develop, and it helps adults to relax. It provides therapy to the fatigued. And since play is pleasurable, and since life needs pleasures, play can be part of a virtuous, happy life. Aristotle explicitly dismisses ascetic and boorish lifestyles that shun pleasure, and he criticizes any life that only works and never experiences leisure. He also denounces any community that demands its citizens always be utilitarian and never experience leisure. This is why he defends *mousikē* as necessary for education. Aristotle judged pleasure and leisure crucial for both individual flourishing and social justice. Play can be part of a flourishing person's leisure time, and it can be part of the appropriate pleasures that people need to live well in larger communities.

On the other hand, we can see the Platonic element in Aristotle's comments on play too. Aristotle warned against pleasures and play. Certain forms of play are expressly forbidden. If the play is base, laborious, or loose, it can habituate a person poorly and lead to unhappiness. Play is never outside the scope of moral considerations for cultivating the best possible self to lead a characteristically good human life. People can play, but only if they also develop the necessary intellectual, ethical, and civic capacities to become full, flourishing humans who help to organize a just society. Additionally, while play cannot be eliminated from life because it helps people to develop and relax, it also cannot be the overall goal of life. Play is not the deepest source of happiness; rather, play serves more serious occupations, like resting one to return to work. We play to gain respite, but we use our renewed minds to attend to deeper matters like cultivating virtuous selves and organizing just communities.

Aristotle's remarks on play are written as though they simultaneously address multiple groups of critics. He wants to defend the importance of play from Spartan communities that may try to eliminate play, leisure, and silliness as superfluous. His defense of play is an accusation against such groups and lifestyles. But he also places limits on play, arguing against critics that may turn the whole of life into a game or a pursuit of the longest and most durable somatic pleasures as the end goal of life. His limitation of play's importance lambasts the wanton, libertine, and luxurious. Play serves the mind, the cultivation of character, and the actualization of the best human lives and communities. Play is not the end of life itself.

Like human life and ethical values, play is complicated for Aristotle. Play is necessary and can help us to overcome temptations to work too hard or to neglect leisure altogether. But play also needs to be evaluated as an action that can deteriorate moral life. It seems appropriate, then, that Aristotle calls play a *pharmakon*, a "drug," translatable as both "medicine" and "poison." His remarks display a philosopher trying to get the dosage of the medicine of play right.

Notes

1. Heraclitus, *Fragments* (Toronto: University of Toronto Press, 1987), B52. The translation is my own. Thanks to Noah Greenstein for reminding me of this fragment. Friedrich Nietzsche echoes this sentiment two millennia later when writing, "A man's maturity—consists in having found again the seriousness one had as a child, at play." *Beyond Good and Evil*, trans. Walter Kaufmann (New York: Vintage, 1989), p. 83.
2. Plato, *Republic*, trans. G. M. A. Grube, rev. C. D. C. Reeve, in: *Plato: The Complete Works*, ed. John M. Cooper (Indianapolis: Hackett, 1997), bk. X.
3. For a discussion of Zeus's forms, see: Dwayne A. Meisner, *Orphic Tradition and the Birth of the Gods* (Oxford: Oxford UP, 2018), pp. 134–6.
4. Much of this was preserved in oral traditions, captured by Homer. But it is also seen in Greek pottery as in: "Vase Number 301645," *Musée du Louvre*, image hosted on beazley.ox.ac.uk.
5. Euripides, *Grief Lessons: Four Plays*, trans. Anne Carson (New York: New York Review Book, 2006).
6. Jacques Derrida also noted the dual meaning of *pharmakon* in: *Dissemination*, trans. Barbara Johnson (Chicago: University of Chicago Press, 1981).
7. These are the translations as offered by: *The Pocket Oxford Classical Greek Dictionary*, ed. James Morwood and John Taylor (Oxford: Oxford University Press, 2002). See also: *A Greek-English Lexicon*, ed. Henry George Liddell, Robert Scott, and Henry Stuart Jones, as uploaded to *Perseus Digital Library*, ed. Gregory R. Crane: http://www.perseus.tufts.edu/hopper/.
8. I owe Jerry Green for discussing with me these terms in the context of Greek education.
9. For discussions of leisure in Aristotle, see: Friedrich Solmsen, "Leisure and Play in Aristotle's Ideal State," *Rheinisches Museum für Philologie*, vol. 107, no. 3 (1964): pp. 193–22; Pierre Destrée, "Education, Leisure, and Politics," in: *The Cambridge Companion to Aristotle's Politics*, eds. Marguerite Deslauriers and Pierre Destrée (Cambridge: Cambridge University Press, 2013), ch. 12. Both notice an ambiguity in Aristotle's use of *scholē*. Sometimes he uses it as free time, others as autotelic activity (activities that we pursue for their own sakes). Though worth noting, it does not affect my argument.
10. Aristotle's arguments imply that any profession that practically eliminates leisure and play prevents its members from flourishing, and organizations bear a responsibility to protect leisure and play. For example, Goldman Sachs limited their daily working hours for interns to 17 after Bank of America Merrill Lynch intern Moritz Erhardt died of an epileptic seizure that might have been triggered by working 72 hours straight. Rupert Neate, "Goldman Sachs Restricts Intern Workday to 17 Hours in Wake of Burnout Death," *The Guardian* (17 June 2015): https://www.theguardian.com/business/2015/jun/17/goldman-sachs-interns-work-hours. Also,

medical residents in the United States are generally limited to working 80-hour weeks, averaged over a few weeks. It is not clear whether these guidelines are adhered to. Morally speaking, Aristotle would find these cases suspect.

11 Noteworthy is Aristotle's discussion of taking a joke. For Aristotle, witty people not only *make* jokes in conversation, sometimes at the expense of others and themselves. Rather, they also *take* jokes made at their expense. A witty person can fail to be witty if she takes too few jokes (or if she accepts every joke about herself). A witty person makes jokes, takes jokes, and also shuts down situations if they seriously harm anyone's honor. Aristotle offers the advice that, when figuring out what the witty thing to do or say is, one should aim to amuse the perfectly witty person, not necessarily one's audience (*EN* 1128a1-2, *EE* 1234a5-23). Similar patterns of play behavior affecting social standing exist in other species, such as howler monkeys. Higher-status monkeys use play as a way of keeping lower-status monkeys in line. In play, they can show how powerful they are while also not hurting their subordinates. Primatologists Sergio and Vivien Pellis liken this to a boss being able to tell a well-placed joke that reminds everyone who is in charge without resorting to totalitarian brutality or making people uncomfortable. *The Playful Brain: Venturing to the Limits of Neuroscience* (Oxford: Oneworld, 2009), p. 146.

12 Diogenes Laertius, *Lives of Eminent Philosophers*, trans. Pamela Mensch (Oxford: Oxford University Press, 2018), V.1–10.

13 I substitute "leisure" for "peace" in the standard translation because it better fits *scholazein*.

14 Hesiod, *Works and Days* in: *Theogony* and *Works and Days*, trans. M. L. West (Oxford: Oxford World Classics, 2008), p. 42.

15 Hesiod, *Works*, p. 46.

16 Solmsen, "Leisure;" Benjamin K. Hunnicutt, "The History of Western Leisure" in: *A Handbook of Leisure Studies*, eds. Chris Rojek, Susan M. Shaw, and A.J. Veal (New York: Palgrave Macmillan, 2006), ch. 4.

17 Aristotle argues that one's leisure time should be spent in contemplative activity like philosophy (*EN* 1177b4-15ff). Leisure itself does not consecrate whatever activity that a person chooses to perform during that time. He clearly prejudices intellectual capacities, such as those used in *theōria*. For a general discussion, see: Destrée, "Education." Though I do think there is a tendency to over-intellectualize Aristotle.

18 Aristotle's remarks on restricting access to art continue a long tradition of Greek thinkers who call into question the public role of gods, athletes, and poetry. Xenophanes, for example, deplored that athletes held greater esteem than sages in the ancient world, and he found it ridiculous that Greeks would worship Olympian gods who are immoral, full of human flaws, and fragmented in their principles. Patricia Curd, ed. *A Presocratics Reader: Selected Fragments and Testimonia*, trans. Richard D. McKirahan and Patricia Curd, 2nd Ed. (Indianapolis: Hackett, 2011), pp. 31–8.

19 Contemporary psychology supports Aristotle's remark about the power of first impressions with its studies on the focusing effect, anchoring effect, and similar cognitive biases that show that people will make decisions based on the first piece of information they have. See: Amos Tversky and Daniel Kahneman, "Judgment under Uncertainty: Heuristics and Biases," *Science*, New Series, vol. 185, no. 4157 (27 Sept. 1974): pp. 1124–31; and Dan Ariely, George Loewenstein, and Drazen Prelec, "Tom Sawyer and the Construction of Value," *Journal of Economic Behavior & Organization*, vol. 60 (2006): pp. 1–10.

20 See: Soraya Nadia McDonald, "Audio of Bill Cosby Joking about Drugging Women Resurfaces," *The Washington Post* (18 Nov. 2014): https://www.washingtonpost.

com/news/morning-mix/wp/2014/11/18/audio-of-bill-cosby-joking-about-drugging-women-resurfaces/; Melena Ryzik, Cara Buckley, and Jodi Kantor, "Louis C.K. Is Accused by 5 Women of Sexual Misconduct," *The New York Times* (9 Nov. 2017): https://www.nytimes.com/2017/11/09/arts/television/louis-ck-sexual-misconduct.html.
21 I substitute "play" here for "amusement" in the original translation. Aristotle's remark at *Rhet.* 1370b31-1371a8 seems also to imply that if a person is forced to play, it cannot be pleasurable. Something about compulsion and bringing an action under the purview of necessity removes the pleasure. Whether or not this transforms the playful event into something else (e.g., non-play or work) is unclear.
22 See: Bernard Suits, "Words on Play," *Journal of the Philosophy of Sport*, Appendix I: Presidential Address, vol. 4, no. 1 (1977): pp. 117–31, who focuses on autotelic activity, doing things for their own sake and not others. See also: Michael Ridge: "Why So Serious? The Nature and Value of Play," *Philosophy and Phenomenological Research*, vol. 105, no. 2 (Sept. 2022): pp. 406–434, who includes fun as essential to play. See: C. Thi Nguyen, *Games: Agency as Art* (Oxford: Oxford University Press, 2020), pp. 114–20, who discusses whether disinterest in a player is similar to disinterest in aesthetic experiences (and see Michael Ridge's reply: "Fun and (Striving) Games: Playfulness and Agential Fluidity," *Journal of the Philosophy of Sport*, vol. 48, no. 3 (2021): pp. 403–13). Lastly, leisure studies raise similar concerns in their debates on defining "leisure." This book defines leisure as free time, but others have defined it as certain activities or elements of subjective experience. See: Johan Bouwer and Marco van Leeuwen, *Philosophy of Leisure: Foundations of a Good Life* (New York: Routledge, 2017).
23 Aristotle also includes, under temperance, a sub-category of softness and endurance. The "soft" person [*malakos*] can neither endure pain nor resist pleasures that most people can (*EN* 1150b16-17). In *EN* VII.7, Aristotle distinguishes different ways of pursuing too many pleasures. The impetuous [*propeteia*] and the weak [*astheneia*] differ considerably. Impetuous people rush toward any pleasure without deliberation, whereas weak people deliberate whether they should pursue pleasures but are overcome by passion or desire. The attention to sub-species of temperance further proves Aristotle's concern for regulating pleasures in a good life.
24 Unfortunately, the surgeon example is true. See: Jonathan Edwards, "A Transplant Surgeon Used an Electric Beam to Burn His Initials into Patients' Organs. He Just Lost His Medical License." *The Washington Post* (31 Jan. 2022): washingtonpost.com.
25 The terms at *Pol.* 1336a29-30 are difficult to translate, so I have offered some rough synonyms instead of quoting a specific translator. Especially in the word *aneleutheros*, Aristotle distinguishes proper play of freemen and citizens from the base, vulgar play and amusement of slaves and commoners. This point is stressed when Aristotle warns that children should be left as little as possible with slaves because slaves misbehave and children can pick up their bad habits (*Pol.* 1336a39-41). It is impossible to erase the social implications these terms had for the audience in ancient Greece. And today, such casual elitism deserves derision.
26 If we judged the importance of play by what tyrants do, it would stress playful pleasures as vital. But Aristotle admits that it indicates little about the value of play that despots value it. Just as boys value different things than men, good people value different things than bad people. So, it is not enough to generalize based on the experience of despots or various rulers; one must also consider the quality of the judge (*EN* 1176b14-25).

27 There is a puzzle here about how to square two remarks by Aristotle on play. On the one hand, he says that play is pleasurable because it lacks necessity (*Rhet.* 1370a12-15). But on the other hand, he also says that we play so that we can get back to work later (*EN* 1176b32-3), meaning that play serves a larger purpose. In other words, subjectively, a player cannot be concerned with necessity, or the play is not play. But (objectively?) the player cannot forsake serious things altogether, or else the player is childish or foolish. Play cannot be the ultimate purpose that our leisure fulfills, which was secured by all our work and maybe even war.

2 Aristotle on Being Happy, Virtuous, and (Maybe) Playful

Room for Playfulness in Aristotle

Maybe there was one time where I dressed myself in a Nacho Libre luchador mask and my dog in a taco costume, and maybe we played fetch throughout my house while I spoke to her in Spanish. While that action might give you some indication of who I am and how I interact with the world, it would give you *much more* information if you knew I did this, hypothetically, at the beginning of every month after I watched *Nacho Libre*, again. There is a fundamental difference between one-time actions and repeated actions that turn into habits and ways we automatically interact with the world. These dispositions that describe how we consistently act throughout our lives are called "character traits." And Aristotle largely pioneered their philosophical study.

As we saw in the previous chapter, Aristotle had a lot to say about play as an action. But he had nothing to say about playfulness as a virtue (a moral character trait). I think this is strange, given how much he talked about play. So, this chapter speculates about how Aristotle *might* have talked about playfulness, even though he did not.

Two quick notes on terminology. First, philosophers sometimes differentiate "ethical" and "moral" in precise ways. Usually, they relate *ethical* to wider-scope considerations about who a person is, what kind of life she leads, and the social situations she faces. These macro-level concerns are used to contextualize what a person does. Whereas *moral* tends to delve into principles, norms, or other subjective things surrounding individual actions and the obligations they generate. The moral tends to be focused on the micro level. However, I use the terms interchangeably, despite judging the ethical almost always more important. Technically, I am doing *virtue ethics* here, and I think "ethical" is a more accurate term in this context. But the contemporary literature about character is located in the field of "moral psychology" and calls traits "moral character traits," so I will use "moral" too.[1]

Second, and even more importantly, the distinction between *playfulness* and *play* is crucial to maintain here. Play is just an action. Playfulness is a virtue. And like any virtue, *playfulness* is a moral character trait. A person develops a character trait through repeated action that forms a disposition. Basically, we as humans face certain situations repeatedly throughout our lives, and our repeated responses to these situations engrain into us patterns of thinking, feeling, and doing. Character traits are psychologically holistic attributes about who a person is and what she values. Character traits involve knowledge, emotion, and motivation. In our case, a playful person is not only someone who plays on one occasion. She plays consistently and well throughout her life. Additionally, she does not play against her will or in inappropriate contexts. Rather she knows when to play, feels good about playing well, and is motivated to play well in any relevant context. The play (or any action relevant to playfulness) is done intentionally, and so it reflects who she is.

But playfulness is not merely a character trait; it is a *moral* character trait, a *virtue*. I am making a much stronger claim than saying playfulness merely describes a person. Character traits in the weak, non-moral sense describe how a person consistently dresses, speaks, moves, etc., as in a novel or script. Non-moral traits might tell us tendencies about a character but pass few judgments and indicate little about how well that person's life is going. For example, knowing that my neighbor likes to wear the color black and listen to The Misfits will not necessarily tell me whether she is a good person. Those character traits do describe her, but they have little to do with her moral characteristics. By contrast, I am going beyond mere descriptions and toward passing judgments when I talk about *moral* character traits or *virtues* and *vices*. I am saying playfulness is a *virtue*, which for me, means that any person possessing this character trait has a better chance at living a full, flourishing human life. Inversely, without developing playfulness, people cannot live that full, characteristically good, human life.[2] Returning to my neighbor, if I found out that she spent her Sunday afternoons for the past few years visiting the elderly in my neighborhood to see if they needed help with any chores, this would indicate that she is a good person (in at least some respects). Similarly, for me, knowing that someone is playful tells us much more about her than knowing only that she prefers the game *ToeJam and Earl* to *Super Mario World*. While not morally neutral, *actions* of play have lower moral stakes than fully developed *moral character traits* like playfulness. Watching fine cinema starring Jack Black on a random Saturday afternoon is judged differently than taking every possible opportunity to do so, with both you and your dog in costume.

As you might guess from my examples and tone, I am not limiting myself to Aristotle's extant words. I am speculating about playfulness by extrapolating *from* things that Aristotle definitively said *to* things that

Aristotle on Being Happy, Virtuous, and (Maybe) Playful 31

I think he might say (but did not). Even though I move from strict exegesis of Aristotle to novel applications of his ideas in this chapter, there are a few good reasons to do this. This is not merely speculation, though it involves some.

First, Aristotle realized that his ethical works could not handle every topic for every audience on every occasion. He placed several limitations on his philosophy. Concerning his audience, he acknowledged that he addressed a limited set of Greek citizens, relying on them to share a common moral education and fill in details where necessary (*EN* 1103b23-5). Concerning his subject matter, he explicitly constrained his subject to *action*, remarking that he was unconcerned with systematic rules for deliberation and precise ways to predicate qualities like goodness. He was content to offer outlines about ethics because he wanted to understand the ethical phenomena in his community in a practical way (*EN* 1096b30-2, 1098a26-9, 1103b36-4a6). And concerning his method, he famously said,

> For it is the mark of an educated person to look for precision in each class of things just so far as the nature of the subject admits … it is evidently equally foolish to accept probable reasoning from a mathematician and to demand from a rhetorician demonstrative proofs.
> (*EN* 1094b24-7)

In other words, wise people understand that the standards for evidence change depending on what the conversation is about. In math, we should expect tight proofs, not just pretty words. In ethics, however, no such standard can be achieved, so we are left with analyzing how actual people live, what the opinions of people are, and whether we think the values under consideration help us to live up to our human potential and lead worthwhile lives. The way that Aristotle added caveats to his conversation shows that he did not take his works to be the be-all, end-all take.

Second, circumstances can change considerably, and when we evaluate things, we might not initially have the exact words that we need to make our points clear. Being wise to his limits, Aristotle left his system open to addition. One bit of evidence for his openness is that he explicitly mentions that certain virtues and vices are *nameless*, or in the Greek *anōnymos* (*EN* 1107b30-2, 1127a13-9). We often understand that changing our character in certain ways can impact whether we live well, even though we do not always have words for the traits that we develop.[3] Aristotle uses courage to illustrate this phenomenon. People who face fear well are deemed "courageous." People who feel too much fear on too many occasions are called "cowardly." But what do we call people who do not feel fear at all, for whom fear is never a factor in calculations when deciding what to do? If such people rush into action, we might call them "rash" or "reckless." But if they are not prone to action, we have no word for them—these tranquil few who are unafraid in all circumstances (*NE* 1107b1-4) yet resist the urge to say "Hold my beer" before departing for foolishness. Human personalities are complicated, and Aristotle allows for the amendment of his system to capture such complexity. He himself did not have words to describe each and every way that humans develop themselves, and he knew that he was starting an ongoing conversation, not a complete and closed catalogue of all human possibilities.

Third, Aristotle is explicit about the fact that experience is the primary content of our ethical systems. Because experiences change, ethics changes. Ethics, for Aristotle, is not an *a priori* exercise in finding immutable, absolute, universal truths about goodness or rightness, divorced from anyone's experience. Ethics, for Aristotle, is about becoming a good person and living a good life in the here and now. And you cannot do that if you do not understand how the world works and how you might fit into it. The role of experience is so important for Aristotle's ethics that he argues that young people are not good at studying ethics or politics precisely because they lack experience (*NE* 1095a3-4). Aristotle prioritizes experience in his ethical method. People thinking about character and the good life must draw on the lived experiences of themselves and others, and changes in this experiential data will change ethical theories. Aristotle acknowledges that there are gaps in his system and that experience will change the considerations.

These remarks lead me to think that there might be room in Aristotle's system for playfulness, even though he himself named no such trait. But to call playfulness a virtue, or a good moral character trait, we need to understand what virtues are and how they interact with happiness, both for Aristotle and for myself as an Aristotelian. And that is the goal of this chapter: to explain fundamental concepts in Aristotelian ethics. I hope that explaining them can show you how Aristotle's ethical system works and why playfulness might be compatible with Aristotle's traditional virtues, such as courage, temperance, wisdom, and justice.

Happiness and Virtues in Aristotle

Why Happiness Matters

We all want to be happy (*eudaimōn*), or so Aristotle assumes. Unlike Plato, who dedicates the first part of *Republic* to combatting moral skepticism and *realpolitik*, Aristotle takes it as given that his readers want to live good lives and be good people. Insofar as we are human animals with healthy, functioning minds, we want to be happy (*DA* 425a10, 432b20-6; *EN* 1099b18-9). For him, the central debate about happiness is not whether we want it; we do.[4] The fundamental debate surrounds the *definition* of happiness (*EN* I.4-5).

To begin his argument, Aristotle surveys the extant views on happiness in ancient Greece. Common people hold that happiness is pleasure; it is a life of consumption. Citizens—people who own land and vote—think that happiness is honor; it is a political life reaping the benefits of good reputation. And philosophers think that happiness is something intellectual, belonging to the best parts of our souls when contemplating theoretical truths. Yet other people think that happiness consists in wealth, good fortune, or virtue (*EN* I.5, I.8).

In setting out the available views on happiness, Aristotle does two things. First, he avoids questions about whether happiness is important by showing that most people already acknowledge its significance. People have opinions about what happiness is, thus, showing that they care. Additionally, nothing theoretical diminishes the practical importance of conversations about happiness. For example, neither the inherent imprecision in ethico-political debates nor deep disagreements keep us from having productive conversations. Whatever the theory, people literally live and die by their ideas of happiness, for example, as when people value and pursue wealth at all costs (*EN* 1094b17-19). What further proof would Aristotle need for the critic who says that these debates do not matter? And even if we cannot prove definitively what happiness is, how can this undermine how relentlessly people pursue it?[5] Aristotle would simply show that some people live well while others suffer due to the paths that they have charted on their maps of the good life.

Second, in surveying extant views on happiness, Aristotle acknowledges that somatic and external goods are important to someone who wants to live a good life. *Somatic goods* are goods relating to the body, such as health and beauty. *External goods* are things such as wealth, honor, friends, and the political circumstances we live in—things entirely separate from our bodies. Most people want some part of health, money, reputation, and meaningful connections to their communities. Without health, people experience debilitating pain. Without money, people writhe in poverty. Without friends, people cannot socialize, receive help, or pursue complex and edifying projects that require cooperation. And without reputation, power, or justice, people experience scorn, vulnerability, and oppression. This in no way entails that people must be gorgeous, wealthy, popular, and in perfect circumstances to flourish. Aristotle explicitly says that we only need moderate amounts of somatic and external goods. Instead, this observation laments that the ugly, poor, lonely, and powerless will struggle more in life than the beautiful, wealthy, beloved, and powerful (*EN* I.5, I.8, 1178b34-1179a9; *Pol.* VII.1).[6] If we have access to somatic and external goods, it makes life better than if we do not.

Unfortunately, health, beauty, wealth, and political circumstances are outside of our control; they are largely a matter of luck. But, for Aristotle, these differences in luck affect how virtuous we can be or how happy we can become. Human life involves luck, and our happiness and virtue are vulnerable to misfortune. By acknowledging the role of external goods, Aristotle concedes partial truth to his opponents. Even if happiness is more than wealth, power, pleasure, or reputation, it certainly involves them, as happiness is easier to accomplish with their aid. Aristotle thus runs a somewhat conciliatory program that integrates many views on happiness into his own. But his on-the-ground observation that people already prefer some lives to others allays the attacks of critics who demand theoretical precision when it has no practical impact. No matter your theoretical persuasion, if given an option about what kind of life you could live, you would choose one with beauty, health, wealth, honor, and justice rather than one without these things. These are not matters of indifference.

What Happiness Is

It cannot be overemphasized that "happiness" for Aristotle differs radically from our contemporary, colloquial use of the term. "Happiness" today is often associated with a short-term emotional state of a person, as when *feeling* happy. But for Aristotle, "happiness" was a *long-term accomplishment* of an entire life lived well, a complete life lacking nothing important. In short, Aristotle defines happiness as a life of virtue and reason (*EN* 1098a18-20, 1099b26-7). For Aristotle, one could feel miserable after illness, divorce, or loss but still be considered happy. This is because happiness transcends mere feelings. Instead, happiness is an ascribed quality of people who have developed themselves in the best possible ways and led full, flourishing, human lives. Happiness is a long-term accomplishment, not a short-term sensation, emotion, or mood.

For Aristotle, happiness is the most purely intrinsic good in life. We pursue it solely based on its own merits and without appeal to anything else. We do not choose happiness because we want pleasure, honor, wealth, or anything else; we choose it for its own sake (*EN* 1097b1-7). Everything else in life, by contrast, is at least partially instrumental or chosen because it helps to accomplish some other task. Why do we want money? It buys bean burritos, nice apartments, or the feeling of security that comes from a retirement fund. The money serves goals other than its mere possession. Why do we want happiness? We just do. And it needs no other justification for its pursuit. This feature of intrinsicness provides a deliberative function too. When uncertain about what to do, we can ask ourselves what would add to our lives in this deep way—a way that makes our lives complete. Not sure whether to take the new promotion, but certain that it will add much more stress and take away time from your loved ones? Aristotle would advise that if you did not need the money, you should prefer your friends, family, and time because they contribute more to your flourishing than the money would in this case. The pursuit of money needs justification in ways that the pursuit of happiness does not.

Happiness is central to Aristotle's ethics, largely due to its unique qualities. Compared to other goods in life such as wealth, health, reputation, and luck, happiness is the most architectonic (*EN* 1094a15), the highest of all goods of action (1095a15-20), the most complete (1097a30), and the best, most noble, and most pleasant (1099a24-5). Moreover, it does not change with a person's circumstances (1095a20-30,1100b15-1101a10). It belongs to a person alone (1095b26). Once achieved, it is hard to take away (1101a9-10; 1100b20-35) and nearly incorruptible (1100b20-1, b31-3, b35). Happiness is self-sufficient (1097b8; 1177a27). It is even more steadfast and stable than knowledge (1100b12-14), a surprising admission from a philosopher. Happiness is the best of all goods in life, and it is the most durable. It seems of a different sort than money or reputation, and compared to money or reputation, happiness weathers misfortune better.

So how do we achieve happiness? It requires many things. Like plants, we humans must develop as healthy entities, nourishing ourselves and growing (*EN* 1098a1-2). Like animals, we must perceive and interact with the world around us, often forming desires and moving toward their fulfillment (1098b25 ff). But unlike plants and animals, we must learn to cultivate the self (1099b18-19), act according to reason (1098a13-14), and act according to virtue (1098a18-20). Human happiness relies on mental capacities that non-humans lack (as far as we can tell). Happy people set themselves the life-long project of becoming the best that they can. They use their reason to train their emotions, motivations, and dispositions to act virtuously on a consistent basis (*EN* I.7-8).

But how do we know what leads to the best development of ourselves? Here, Aristotle grounds happiness in the function of human animals (*EN* I.7). He makes two central claims about human happiness. First, happiness needs to be something distinct (*idion*) about humans compared to other living things (1098a1). This rules out nutrition, growth, perception, action, and desire because plants and animals can do these things too. *Human* happiness requires something more, even though it certainly includes aspects of life that we share with plants and animals. Second, in looking for the distinct human function, Aristotle wants to find the quality that generalizes to *all* happy people. He analogizes humans to cithara players. If cithara players can be defined as a group as those who play the cithara well, humans must have some similar function that defines them. Aristotle thinks that this common capacity for happy people is the activity of the mind according to virtue (1098a17-18). And whenever people cultivate their minds to lead a life according to virtue, they fulfill their human function the best, and therefore, they lead happier lives. Consistently, Aristotle argues that the best things, the highest pleasures, and the most durable goods are those that perfect us, those that help us to achieve our highest purpose, our *telos*.[7] This is what Aristotle thinks our reason and character do. If people develop their minds and create good habits to respond to life's challenges, then they live as well as humanly possible. Cultivated minds live excellently.

Happiness, therefore, is not an acquired product or an isolated action, nor is it a mere state of mind. Happiness is a deep cultivation of one's capacities to develop the uniquely human attributes that lead to a flourishing human life. It involves the careful management of the many things that we care about—health, wealth, friends, family, career, social standing, etc. By living according to reason and cultivating virtues, people have the best chance of achieving happiness. The goal is to become good people and lead good lives. Good character, good living, and the goods of life mutually reinforce each other.

Why We Need Virtues for Happiness

For Aristotle, people want to be happy, and they can be happy only by fulfilling their specific function as human animals: living a life according to virtue (*EN* 1098a18-20,1099b26-7). Virtues, therefore, are necessary components of being a happy person. They are part of what defines a good human, and they are common to all happy people. Those who develop the virtues become better people and lead better lives as a result (*EN* II.7).[8]

Aristotle is quick to emphasize that the virtues are natural capacities (*dynameis*). But by natural capacities, he does not mean they develop automatically. If people were automatically im/moral, they would be unable to change, and this would confound moral instruction and correction. Yet just because it takes work to develop virtues does not mean that it goes against some rigid human nature. Training someone to become good is not foolish in a way that training a rock to fall upward is. Aristotle contrasts virtues with our senses. We use sight or smell because we have them, but virtues are things that we have because we use them. Both are natural, but they are developed in different ways. People develop their capacities for character into actuality through moral education and self-cultivation (*EN* 1103a27-9). Virtues are developed through proper forms of habituation (*EN* II.1). This comes out especially in the Greek word for virtue, *aretē*. Not only can we translate it as "virtue" but also as "excellence." Virtues are excellent ways of being, especially with respect to common experiences, situations, and goods that all humans interact with.

Aristotle connects virtues to situations that all humans face. You can think of virtues as psychological tools that specialize to work on each situation *uniquely*. For every situation or emotion that humans face that will impact their ability to flourish significantly, there is an Aristotelian virtue that helps regulate it. For example, because we all face fear, we need a virtue of courage. Because we all face pleasure, we need a virtue of temperance. Or because we all have access to goods, we need a virtue of generosity (*EN* II.7). Virtues regulate emotions or situations in life that all human animals face universally.[9] And happy people need to develop the virtues to face these situations well. Whether we want to or not, we repeatedly face these situations and develop habits toward them. If we develop good characters, we stand a chance at flourishing; if we develop bad characters, flourishing becomes impossible. For example, if we cower in fear, we never learn new things, ask cute people to dinner, or go up for promotions. If pleasure rules our lives and we can never say no to any pleasure, we watch our relationships and careers crumble in the face of sensual delights. If we are greedy, we never help others, and others rightly hate us for our callousness toward them. The Aristotelian claim is that our lives are worse if we do not develop the virtues.

But trying to understand what someone should do in a situation is difficult. For example, we may know that we must face fear, and that courage helps us to face that fear well. But how much fear is tolerable, and what should we do in a given situation? To define virtues, Aristotle employs a heuristic: "the mean between the extremes," the spot between excess and deficiency. Aristotle compares calculating how to be virtuous to finding the center of a circle or hitting the bullseye of a target: it is difficult and relies on skill, and there are many ways of going wrong, but by knowing the excesses, we can aim between them to find the center. After all, the center of a circle is equidistant from all parts of its boundaries. The analogy places proper development of a trait as equidistant from its malformed extremes. For example, take courage when facing fear. Being overwhelmed by fear, in excess, will lead to cowardice because someone gives in to fear too easily. But having no fear and disregarding it entirely, deficiency, will lead to foolhardiness because someone who never heeds fear rushes into hopeless situations. Both too much and too little regard for fear destroy the virtue of courage; excess and deficiency destroy excellent being and action (*EN* II.2). Courage lies somewhere in the middle. So, in cases where the right thing to do is not obvious, sometimes it helps to consider the wrong things. Then you can find the sweet spot between the extremes of action.

At their most basic level, virtues are dispositions. The Greek word *hexis* connotes that a person's disposition is a deep feature of her character and nearly unalterable (contrasting with *schesis*, which is a more easily changeable state). A dispositional quality is something that someone has unflinchingly. This is easiest to see in negative examples, perhaps as with someone who has the disposition of loving alcohol. If fully developed into a disposition, this person will never turn down a drink, no matter if sated or drunk. Part of something being a disposition is that it is a fully developed trait that is hard to undo (or improve upon in more positive cases). Of course, character traits vary according to how developed they are, and they can be stunted or misapplied such that they hinder living well. But once the character trait has reached the level of a disposition, it is set and arduous to change (*EN* II.5, 7). The difficulty to change dispositions is why Aristotle and many of the Greeks stress the importance of moral education. Aristotle says a good education makes all the difference in the world (*EN* 1103b23-5). It is difficult to change in adulthood what has been set in the two decades prior.

To form, dispositions require repeated work of a person's entire psychology. They are developed with intent, and actions flowing from a virtue must be decided by the actor and done knowingly (*EN* 1150a31-5). Virtues are not developed by mere chance or compulsion. Rather, they are developed on purpose and are an extension of a person's agency. Aristotle contrasts virtues with skills (*technai*). Whereas skills only need knowledge, virtues need knowledge, decisiveness, and consistency. This gets Aristotle around the possibility that someone could become happy or virtuous by accident. In the same way that someone who inadvertently spells a complicated word correctly is not a scholar, someone who accidentally does something courageous is not a hero. To be courageous, in the Aristotelian sense, is to have decided to develop the disposition to act courageously and to have developed that trait to fullness over time. A courageous person knows herself and what she can handle. She knows which things in her life and community will most likely inspire fear. She can feel that fear without it overwhelming her, and she does not try to suppress it. She can give an account of why she acts and what she feels when acting. And her life chronicles her psychological development with respect to fear, the many occasions when she has failed and triumphed over fear. A fully courageous person is guided by reason but has an intimate familiarity with her emotions and habits. She puts in the work of understanding and developing her whole self and putting that self into action.

Feelings and manner of execution matter to virtue too (*EN* 1106b36-7a9). The actor cannot begrudge the right action. People must feel good about doing good things and feel bad about doing bad things or making mistakes. The virtuous are the test of virtues, and it is not enough merely to imitate their actions (though that is how we all begin to develop virtues). Rather, we must also feel the way that they feel, and we must do things in the ways that they do things. Meaning, the goal is to do good things with lucid thought and fluid emotions and unconflicted motivations (*EN* II.3-4). The virtuous make virtuous action look easy, and that is where we want to get eventually too. Intent, fluidity, and tact matter. For example, the homeless community in Nashville creates and sells a newspaper called *The Contributor*, and the sales help the homeless vendors and community. Buying a newspaper from a homeless person with a hardened heart and an angry thrust of the money toward the vendor does some good (it does buy a paper), but it is not generous. A generous person would feel unconflicted about buying the newspaper, and she would treat the vendor with decency and kindness. To be virtuous, a person cannot merely know what to do and execute an action; she must also feel appropriately about what she does and execute the action appropriately.[10] To be fully virtuous goes beyond achieving a result or setting the right intentions. Manner of execution matters, and everything about the virtuous person is unified toward acting well—thoughts, feelings, and life goals.

So, Aristotle argues that we all want to be happy and that happiness is the distinctly human life lived fully and well. It is a life of nutrition and growth; motion and desire; and reason and virtue. Each aspect contributes to fulfilling our human function of living with excellence. The virtues are just the cultivated natural capacities that bring us closer to happiness when interacting with unavoidable aspects of life. They are dispositions to act knowledgeably, decisively, and consistently, and they generate actions that are sensitive to feelings and tact. Good people lead good lives.

How to Find a Virtue in Three Easy Steps

So now we know what happiness and virtues are for Aristotle. But what does this have to do with play? Do all good people play? Can we imagine someone who lives the most complete life and who has developed the most exemplary of human characters but does not, at least on occasion, play a game with friends, or go out to a movie, or maybe hire an *elotero* to serve Mexican street corn at a watch party of *Nacho Libre* that he throws for his family and friends?

For Aristotle, the answer is clear: no such person exists. All good people play. In the previous chapter, we saw how he specifically defended that children ought to play because it helps their bodies and minds to develop and that adults use play to rest from daily labors (*Pol.* VII-VIII; *EN* X.6). Perhaps his clearest statement was that he closed his grandest political treatise by arguing that the fully just community will educate its citizens not only in practical things, such as *gramma* (reading and writing) and *graphē* (drawing, diagramming, and drafting). All of those things help people conduct business and coordinate their efforts with others. Aristotle added two more essential subjects to proper education: *gymnasion* (physical training) and *mousikē* (the arts of the Muses, especially music and poetry). He even went as far as to say that states like Sparta or other imperialistic, war-hungry states failed because they did not educate their citizens to be able to live a life of peace and leisure (*Pol.* VII.14). Free people need the *liberal* arts; they must be able to use their leisure time well.

Free people do not spend all their time doing utilitarian things or plotting the next war (*Pol.* VIII.2-3). This, minimally, tells us that Aristotle felt that some instances of play were *morally permissible*, able to be done in a moral life. But I think it actually shows that play is a *necessary* part of any good life, if only developmentally and psychologically. How else can children develop, adults rest, and states have a populace that does not use their free time in destructive manners? And yet, we also saw in the previous chapter that Aristotle felt that only *proper* play is ethically permissible, and even so, proper play cannot be the end goal of life. Vulgar play deserves literal beatings, he argued (*Pol.* VII.17, VIII.6). He also repeatedly exclaimed the absurdity of the idea of spending all our leisure at play (*EN* X.6; *Pol.* VIII.3). Aristotle was of two minds.

Aristotle did little to resolve his ambivalence about play. But after this chapter, we might. We now have the answer as to how he might judge play's value: by relating it to happiness or virtues. He did not do this. But could he?

The immediate and easiest way of potentially judging the ethical value of play would be for Aristotle to relate play to some other virtue. The most likely candidate would be temperance, which helps us regulate our experiences of pleasure and pain. However, I think that this is a bad fit because temperance relates most directly to somatic pleasures, such as eating, drinking, and having sex. The problem is that play of both high- and low-brow varieties seems more complicated than this, even if it involves a fair amount of it. There are many educational and leisure-time activities that we would call play that are not so casual as pleasure-inducing idleness. You can ruin idleness by putting in too much effort. But you cannot ruin leisure-time play through effort, such as practicing your favorite instrument, lifting heavy weights because you like to, or playing your favorite challenging video game. Pleasure, and so temperance, is part of the process, but it seems as though it is too reductive for what is going on in many leisure activities. We can see this, especially if we look at bad examples of play, such as writing racist country songs, giving yourself rhabdomyolysis through overtraining, or yelling slurs at strangers in an online game. Temperance would deem these things unethical in terms of pleasure and pain. But that does not seem to capture the unethical quality here. Aristotle's concerns about immoral play supersede concerns about pleasure and pain. Hypothetically, we might imagine a Jason Aldean-loving CrossFitter who posts racist memes on 4chan's /b/ and shouts gamer words in the *Call of Duty* voice chat as he recovers from rabdo. Such a hypothetical person's moral missteps would go beyond mere mistakes in pleasure and pain.

We could also look at any of Aristotle's other canonical virtues, but none seem like good fits either (see: *EN* II.7). The closest alternative might be wittiness, which regulates social pleasures. But this fails to capture what is happening in the example mentioned above too.

With play, it seems like there is some element of it that directly impacts flourishing. But Aristotle did not connect it with his existing virtues or any other overarching concern. However, we can. My eventual thesis of the book, which is defended in Chapter 4, will be that *playfulness* is a virtue that helps us regulate our leisure time to rest, develop ourselves, and engage our communities. Play can be virtuous if it helps the playful person use her leisure time well.

However, if I want to make this case on consistent Aristotelian grounds, I have to follow the Aristotelian formula. Luckily, after this chapter, you have already seen that, for Aristotle, there are three simple steps to finding out whether a character trait is a virtue.

1 The Eudaimonist Requirement: Make sure that the trait under consideration regulates uniquely an emotion or situation in life that all humans experience that affects whether a person can flourish.
2 The Empirical Requirement: Make sure that the trait under consideration is part of the character of all happy people. Stated differently, make sure that no happy person lacks this trait.
3 The Psychological Requirement: Make sure that the trait under consideration is psychologically complex—involving reason, emotion, motivation, and tact.

If a thinker can find a trait that meets all three requirements, then she has a strong case for why that trait is a virtue on Aristotelian grounds.

My main challenge here is to move from play as an action to playfulness as a character trait. I need to find a universal situation that all humans face that can make or break their happiness. I need to find a trait that all happy people have in common that regulates that situation uniquely. I need to find a trait that admits of psychological complexity, reflecting the intricacies of human character. And to do these things, I examine biology, psychology, sociology, media studies, and philosophy in the next chapter.

Notes

1 For a discussion of actions and narratives, see: Alasdair MacIntyre, *After Virtue*, 3rd ed. (South Bend, IN: University of Notre Dame Press, 2008), ch. 15.
2 I subscribe to eudaimonism. But I must mention that Christine Swanton offers an alternative in her *Target Centered Virtue Ethics* (Oxford: Oxford University Press, 2021).
3 For a discussion of Aristotle's nameless virtues, see: Paula Gottlieb, "Aristotle's 'Nameless' Virtues," *Apeiron*, vol. 27, no. 1. (1994): pp. 1–16.
4 Like Aristotle's argument, mine will not address a moral skeptic or nihilist. However, there is important work being done on whether Aristotle's ethical

theory is compatible with mood disorders. See: Mara Neijzen, "The Accessibility of Moral Virtue in the Context of Depressive Episodes," *The Journal of Ethics*, vol. 27 (2023): pp. 393–414.

5 Aristotle, of course, never considered the possibility of error theories or fictionalism about virtue or happiness, views that would hold that virtue or happiness does not exist, even though our ordinary discourse earnestly tries to refer to them. Contemporarily philosophers do, though. See: Christian B. Miller, *Character and Moral Psychology* (Oxford: Oxford University Press, 2014): ch. 7; Mark Alfano, *Character as Moral Fiction* (Cambridge: Cambridge University Press, 2013): ch. 4.

6 For a discussion on happiness and the downtrodden, see: Matthew Cashen, "The Ugly, the Lonely, and the Lowly: Aristotle on Happiness and the External Goods," *History of Philosophy Quarterly*, vol. 29, no. 1 (Jan. 2012): pp. 1–19.

7 This idea of a purpose, final end, or human function garners much criticism in contemporary ethics, which is largely uncomfortable with saying any such purpose, end, or function exists. See: Bernard Williams, *Ethics and the Limits of Philosophy* (Cambridge, MA: Harvard University Press, 1985), esp. ch. 3; MacIntyre, *After Virtue*, ch. 18.

8 For a discussion of virtues benefitting their possessors, see: Rosalind Hursthouse, *On Virtue Ethics* (Oxford: Oxford UP, 1999), ch. 8.

9 Martha Nussbaum points out this same pattern between spheres of life and virtues in: "Non-Relative Virtues: an Aristotelian Approach," in *Moral Disagreements: Classic and Contemporary Readings*, ed. Christopher W. Gowans (London: Routledge, 2000), pp. 168–71.

10 For an analysis of virtue, see: Julia Annas, "Virtue Ethics," in: *The Oxford Handbook of Ethical Theory*, ed. David Copp (Oxford: Oxford University Press, 2006): ch. 18.

3 Harmonizing the Cacophony of Claims about Play

Everyone sings about play. But they sing different songs simultaneously. Biologists, psychologists, and other scholars have studied play in the 2300 years since Aristotle. This chapter reviews the strange state of the literature on play. I think it is best summarized by biologist Gordon Burghardt:

> Neither inherently useful or useless, neither good nor evil. ... Play may prevent achievement or corrupt lives ... Play may also be something like food, drink, sex, and competition, which are only good in moderation: extremism may not be a virtue in play, although the most valuable or creative play may be extreme. ... We cannot ignore an activity that occupies so much of our lives and directs our goals. We need to wrestle with it; play with it; immerse ourselves in understanding it. The ultimate paradox may be that play can only be understood through itself.[1]

Play is equally alluring and bewildering. People can sense that it needs to be understood, yet it confounds the categories that we most often use to understand things. Basically, despite everything written, people do not know what to do with it. As much as scholars try, few arrive at philosophically precise or ethically attuned conclusions. In fact, many scholars resort to assertions, anecdotes, and peripheral remarks.[2]

Rather than construct arguments out of the fragments, I approach the current research with an Aristotelian strategy. In *On the Soul*, Aristotle parallels non-humans and humans. He extrapolates psychological insights about humans from the ways non-humans grow, reproduce, desire, and think. I wish to do the same for play by examining the biology and psychology of non-human play. The various phenomena involved in non-human play concern what animals do when they do things not immediately related to survival. And yet, human behavior is also unique because humans evoke rationality and abstract values in play. In this chapter, I reconcile the interdisciplinary research on play. This will set up my definition of the virtue of playfulness in the next chapter.

DOI: 10.4324/9781032717722-4

A Cacophony of Claims about Play

Play exercises wondrous powers, at least if we believe its evangelizers. Something about the activity of play reveals the deep nature of the player, as well as the mysteries of life itself. For example, philosopher Moritz Schlick argues, "The meaning of existence is revealed only in play."[3] Games scholar Miguel Sicart intensifies these claims by writing, "Play is a form of understanding what surrounds us and who we are, and a way of engaging with others. Play is a mode of being human."[4] Old proverbs weigh in too with sayings like, "You can discover more about a person in an hour of play than in a year of conversation."[5] So, thinkers connect the activity of play to meaningful human lives. And play, for some, expresses a vital part of human nature.[6]

The hyperbolic claims about play also go beyond individuals and life. Some claim that play is the engine of human civilization and culture. Sociologist Johan Huizinga dedicates *Homo Ludens* to defending one thesis: "For us the whole point is to show that genuine, pure play is one of the main bases of civilization."[7] Historian Steven Johnson echoes this in his book *Wonderland*,

> Everyone knows the old saying 'Necessity is the mother of invention,' but if you do a paternity test on many of the modern world's most important ideas or institutions, you will find, invariably, that leisure and play were involved in the conception as well.[8]

Between Huizinga and Johnson, play is supposedly responsible for human language, civilization, law, war, knowledge, poetry, mythopoeisis, philosophy, art, fashion, shopping, music, gastronomy, technology, games, and public spaces. The activity of play drives humans to develop culture and institutions that have wide-ranging effects.

Philosophers are not immune to this pattern of exaggerated comments about play either. John Wall surveys the history of philosophy to organize philosophers into three camps on play. *Top-down philosophers*—such as Plato, Augustine, Kant, Heidegger, and Gadamer—see play as indicative of childhood, which is vibrant and creative, but also unruly and unreasoned. For them, play must be tamed by rationality, just as children must be civilized by education. By contrast, *bottom-up philosophers*—such as Clement of Alexandria, Rousseau, Schleiermacher, and Derrida—hold that play displays human goodness, authenticity, and spontaneity. For them, the qualities intrinsic to play deserve preservation from childhood onward (rather than taming). Lastly, *developmental philosophers*—such as Aristotle, Aquinas, and Maimonides—see play as a neutral activity that can gradually help individuals and groups to grow.[9] So, for philosophers, play is a tappable power, unacknowledged drive, or useful building block.

Philosophers and scholars think play important to address. But many only do so in passing remarks on the way to bigger points, or it is used as rhetorical flourish to praise or scorn the childlike qualities of a subject. Play and playfulness do not receive the rigor and focused attention that they deserve, especially when compared to the copious literature on art, love, friendship, justice, or other ethical and political topics that receive book-length treatments that get assigned to classes as essential reading. This review is a mere splash from the sea of ink rained from pens celebrating or deriding play. I could add more, but this section should already show the general patterns of claims made about play, erratic as they are.[10] Scholars argue that play should be restrained or indulged, or maybe used in the service of other goals. Play is viewed as a redeemer or a tempter. But little substance buttresses these conclusions. And it is unclear how play gets involved in so many things or why people evaluate it differently.

What Non-Human Play Can Tell Us about Human Play[11]

Philosophers and humanists have debated about play for literally thousands of years. Without much hope for resolution, I want to change focus. I think that the scientists who study play today are making important contributions to this debate, but they are underrepresented in the philosophical literature. In this section, I survey some of the empirical findings relevant to the importance of play in non-humans, especially those by neuroscientists Sergio and Vivien Pellis and biologists Patrick Bateson and Paul Martin.[12] Here, I think that we can gain novel insights into why evaluations of play are so ambivalent.

Everything an animal does has evolutionary stakes. A behavior's benefits must have outweighed its detriments to have developed. Play carries a cost. Relative to rest, it uses energy, risks injury, and draws attention to the player. For example, sea lions are more likely to kill and eat young seals when they play. Or lion cubs tagging along on their mother's hunt may ruin it by play pouncing on each other, making noise, and thus scaring away gazelles.[13] However, despite its risks, play presents opportunities for development. In physical play with objects, peers, or the environment, animals fine-tune their neuromuscular and sensory skills. They learn to use their own bodies in protected situations that simulate complex behaviors. They get practice navigating their complicated worlds and executing intricate maneuvers. Additionally, in social play, animals learn to compete, co-exist, and cooperate with other kin and other species. They learn to confront, acquiesce to, and collaborate with others to accomplish larger goals. Puppies at play do more than chew toys or annoy their siblings; while playing, they learn how to behave under simulated pressure to hunt and fight, and they learn to pounce, jump, run,

46 *Harmonizing the Cacophony of Claims about Play*

and stalk in the terrain around their homes. Additionally, by interacting with other dogs, they learn to recognize their kin, and they learn skills from their peers.[14] Animals can even practice skills via pretending, as when chimpanzees cradle, carry, and care for sticks to practice childrearing. So, despite its risks, play teaches animals by facilitating understanding of the self, community, and environment.[15]

Neuroscientists Sergio and Vivien Pellis survey experiments done with rats to defend play's importance. Rats compete to nuzzle each other's napes by attacking, defending, and adapting to each other's advances.[16] This behavior is ingrained in deep parts of the brain. We know this because when scientists remove the executive functioning parts of the brain, those rats still play and play fairly.[17] But play is not just prevalent behavior; it is crucial to psychological development. Consider experiments done with animals deprived of play. Rats who did not play in their childhood cannot mate or socialize as well as rats who did. Play-deprived rats can move and think like other rats when by themselves, but they appear frightened in interactions with others. This prohibits coordination with partners, as they cannot predict or choreograph movements with others. Never mind attracting a mate; play-deprived rats cannot even mount a mate.[18]

Pellis and Pellis conclude from these experiments that play seems to train an animal's response to stress coming from unpredictable circumstances, especially as exhibited by other animals. Rats who do not play tend to overreact to any playful advance, taking it as an attack. They therefore get into more fights because they misunderstand the behavior of rats around them. And when they actually are attacked by others, they take a longer time to recover from the stress and to return to normal behavior. They cannot cope.[19] This means that play deprivation is brutal, especially in a social species. The daily lives of play-deprived animals involve many failed social interactions that incite high levels of stress. Play-deprived rats fail at friendship and sex.

Healthy rats, by contrast, use play fighting (AKA "rough-and-tumble play") as a means of social cohesion, stress reduction, and maintenance of friendships. By playing to nuzzle each other's napes, healthy rats learn to deal with the stress of confrontation, and they adapt their movements to an unpredictable opponent. This contest bonds them with their play partners. Play thus serves more than the developmental functions of individual, juvenile rats; it serves wider social functions too. Because it regulates stress and fosters community, play behavior continues in rats beyond childhood and into adulthood.[20]

However, while play can be good, excessive play has negative effects. In one experiment that the Pellises discuss, rats were held in large cages with plentiful objects to interact with (as opposed to the normal group raised inside standard cages with only a few things to interact with). The rats who lived in the enriched environment performed worse at sex than normal rats. Other experiments also show that rats raised with excessive opportunities to play do not heed danger. Rather than walking along walls or under cover, they run in the open and explore; they seek novelty. This exposes them to predators. The Pellises' survey of experiments proves one thing: moderate quantities of play are essential for healthy rats.[21] Rats that play excessively spend too much time on diversion rather than developing individual or social skills, and this stunted their social lives and responses to the environment. Moreover, similar evidence is found in studies on primates and other species.[22]

Biologists Patrick Bateson and Paul Martin offer similar analyses of experiments done on animals to assess the importance of play. They agree with the Pellises that play simulates stress in a protected context. But in addition to stress regulation, Bateson and Martin argue that play allows animals to find newer, more optimal solutions to everyday problems. Rather than relying on instinct and social learning to perform mundane tasks, animals that play can create novel, alternative solutions that break them out of less efficient ways of doing things. Bateson and Martin offer a mountain climbing analogy. Sometimes climbers find themselves on a false summit, and it is only after they look around that they realize there is a taller summit elsewhere. In engineering, the false summit is called a "local optimum," and the actual, taller summit is a "global optimum." Play offers the opportunity to animals to assess their own summit to investigate whether more globally optimal patterns of behavior lay elsewhere. Even though convention or habit holds that the current way of doing things is best, play looks elsewhere to make sure. Play provides a space for novel behavior. And while most playful actions might not find more optimal ways of doing things, occasionally play will hit upon a novel, better way. And this can be taken up by any animal that learns the optimal behavior.

Play leading to better ways of doing things has many examples in animal behavior. For one, dolphins sometimes play by blowing rings and bubbles out of their blowholes underwater. Some biologists speculate that this eventually led to dolphins using the bubbles to screen off and move fish to the surface, where dolphins can catch them more easily. Similarly, a group of humpback whales in Alaska has been observed using walls of bubbles to trap fish. They then use loud calls to scare the fish toward the surface.[23] Sometimes play involves seemingly useless things, like teaching animals to blow bubbles to chase or swim through. But other times, the skills learned while playing result in innovations that help animals to survive.[24]

The exploratory features of play, along with its social aspects, allow it to train animals to assess conflicting demands. In keeping up with partners and creating novel solutions, play prepares animals to deal with situations that they were never previously prepared for.[25] While instinct and social learning can anticipate most situations an animal faces, play teaches animals to adapt and assess on-the-fly.

Bateson and Martin also corroborate the Pellises' point that play is a sign of wellbeing in animals. When stressed, hungry, anxious, or ill, animals do not usually play. For example, playing rats will stop if exposed to cat hair. They even stop soliciting play for days afterward. Relatedly, the play of vervet monkeys is correlated with food scarcity. In dry years with scarce food, the monkeys do not play. But in wetter years with plentiful food, the monkeys play, and they play more if compensating for unplayful years. Gelada baboons and meerkats also follow similar patterns with their lack of play during scarcity. This shows play's link to predictable, safe environments. All other things being equal, if animals are provided more safety and predictability, they will play more. This was shown in an experiment with pigs, where the experimental group was given a sound cue each time it was taken to an enriched environment with straw and seeds. Because this group of pigs could reliably predict abundance, they played more than another group of pigs that was also given the same access to the environment but without a sound cue that trained them.[26]

So, what do all these experiments mean? The experiments that the Pellises survey teach us that play helps in the neuromuscular coordination of individual animals with their bodies and their environments, as well as the development of psychological mechanisms that help animals to regulate their emotions when dealing with stress and unpredictable circumstances. Play also helps animals bond and coordinate their behavior with others. Martin and Bateson add to this. They show that play provides simulations of stressful activities, and its protected environments allow animals to rehearse common solutions and explore novel ones. Play is therefore linked to the creative generation of new solutions to problems. And when a group of animals adopts a new behavior to optimize something, it is linked to innovation. But apart from skills, playful behavior indicates that an animal is not overly stressed, hungry, anxious, or ill. Play indicates that an animal feels well, safe, and faces predictable challenges.

There is some hope that insights from these studies apply to humans. In fact, humans are the most playful species with the most complex patterns of play. And humans are famously neotenous, retaining more juvenile qualities into adulthood longer than any other animal.[27] So, it is likely that play serves some biological function for humans and that it involves some of the behavioral aspects that scientists have observed in the play of other animals.

There are many parallels between animal play and human childhood development. The biological evidence supports Aristotle's imperative that young children ought to play instead of work because it helps them learn and develop (*Pol.* VII.17). Biology and psychology prove that juvenile animals must learn to use their bodies during complex behaviors in dynamic environments. They must also learn to coordinate with peers, kin, and other species. Play helps with all of this. In developmental stages, play makes possible the serious and complex tasks of adult life.[28]

Why Human Play and Playfulness Extend beyond Non-Human Play

But the adult world of humans is sufficiently different from childhood or any other animal's life such that the lessons from the previous section might not precisely map on to my book's purpose: finding the virtue of playfulness. We must exercise caution in applying the descriptive work of biology and psychology to the normative work of ethics.[29] It is a much different task to *describe* the behavior of animals accurately, as scientists do, than it is to *prescribe* which types of play should be encouraged or disallowed, as I and other philosophers do. So, I recommend care and attention for a few reasons.

First, play in human adults is much more sophisticated than anything else in the animal world. Non-human animals are wonderous in their complexity, and animals have been observed to play in dozens of ways. For example, a powerful lion may let a weaker lion pounce on it, thus reversing roles. Or a dolphin may take a ball, submerge it, and let it shoot to the surface, thus exhibiting complex play with objects.[30] But neither can compare to what adult humans do in sports like football, games like Catan, entertainment like *The Office*, or imaginative activities like Dungeons and Dragons. It is this complex adult world of play that captures my interest.

Second, in looking for a virtue related to play, I need to find a situation or emotion in life that it can regulate *uniquely*. Courage regulates fear uniquely; temperance regulates somatic pleasures uniquely; wit regulates social amusements uniquely; etc. What, then, would playfulness regulate? Non-human research offers four candidates: neuromuscular training, stress regulation, social coordination, and wellbeing. But all four are poor candidates for human virtue because humans can achieve all four things by means different than play. Playfulness cannot uniquely regulate stress because therapy, meditation, medication, or socializing might work just as well, and those are not necessarily actions of playful people. Similarly, the sphere of playfulness cannot be training neuromuscular coordination, as work or stern, no-frills powerlifting gyms like Westside Barbell could do the same. Social coordination is not unique to playful people, and wellbeing is much broader than playfulness. So, we need to look beyond the functions of play in non-human research in order to understand the uniqueness of human play.[31]

Third, for Aristotle, virtues are constituents of a good life; virtues are necessary conditions for happiness. There is no way to live well without courage, temperance, or wit, for example. In examining the research on play and what it says about virtues and happiness, we might distinguish between *helpful* things and *necessary* things. Play, undoubtedly, is helpful for developing certain virtues or a good life. It helps children develop. It helps adults rest and have fun. It brings people together and forms a community. However, I am asking about its necessity: is it possible for someone to live the best human life and be an exemplary person of character without her ever having played or becoming a playful person? I am looking for a moral character trait necessary for living well, *not* a mere nonmoral character trait, *not* a mere occasional activity that people may undergo but ultimately do not have to. This is why I must go beyond the biological and behavioral sciences because they do not make such strong claims.

A fourth reason chastens hasty application of science to philosophy. Philosophy must supplement biological and psychological studies of play in non-humans because human play includes things that have no analogues in the animal world. In non-humans, play is used to simulate complex or high-stakes behaviors, such as fighting, mating, and feeding. Animals play at these to develop requisite skills for living, and play reduces the intensity of stress associated with these phenomena. The benefits of practice and composure preserve playful behavior for these types of activities. That said, animals do not play at safe activities, such as grooming, urinating, or defecating.[32] Humans do, though. Toddlers regularly mimic behaviors that make their parents blush in polite company. People exaggeratedly swoop their hair back, squirt their mouths with imaginary breath spray, or smooth their eyebrows to signal to their friends that they are about to talk to someone that they find attractive. Colleagues jerk their lightly closed fists back and forth through the air to each other to indicate the triviality of a meeting or the unbearable sanctimony of a person's moralizing. Humans play at and with activities that animals do not.[33]

Part of the uniqueness of human play comes from the fact that humans can add something to play that animals cannot: implicit and explicit values. For example, we can play with taboos to reveal the values that suppress certain behaviors. This begins early in childhood. Toddlers play in purely imaginative, pretend ways by fantasizing adventures, like dragons having a tea party. But around age five, children begin playing in ways that involve making rules, negotiating enforcement, and mimicking the social roles that they see in their communities.[34] Then, dragons do not merely exist as imaginary friends, but they must have wings, and they cannot play with you if you do not show etiquette. Animals cannot do this. They do not have any equivalent to the values invoked in childhood imagination or adult society's parody, mockery, or ritual. To make this point starker, consider jesters and carnivals. Jesters can speak truths that normal citizens cannot, often called a "jester's privilege." They can do so because they are involved in a playful ritual. Relatedly, carnivals can turn a collective of stratified people with sharp castes and power imbalances into a reveling crowd on equal ground. Anthropologists have argued that big events where we participate in and spectate play offer an opportunity for us to see our community's values externalized and for us to see how we react to our values.[35] Love them or hate them, but the Super Bowl and the World Cup show what many people value, and communities show what they value in how they accommodate the events and their spectators. Human play can interact with values, and these forms of play have no equivalent in non-humans.[36]

For humans, play can also be transgressive, and creativity often tests (and sometimes violates) boundaries. Everyone can acknowledge the genius of Goethe and Mozart, but few people today know Goethe's *Götz von Berlichingen*. There, the protagonist responds to an enemy's request for his surrender with: "Me, surrender! Grace and shame! … Tell your captain for His Imperial Majesty, that I, like always, have due respect! But tell him: he can lick me in the ass!"[37] Inspired by this scene, Mozart later composed a canon entitled "Lick Me in the Ass." In many creative, artistic, and playful endeavors, humans uncover, modify, disregard, and transgress values. Some of this is supplemented by humans' uses of humor and thought-play. They do not have to manipulate objects or interact with peers to play; they can do so all in their minds or in language.[38] Goethe and Mozart produced abstract symbols of play. This aspect of play cannot be explained by biological data gathered from non-humans.

In fact, coming together in groups and forming playful spaces have been profound parts of human history. Group activities sometimes create what social scientists call "collective effervescence," a profound and sacred feeling that occurs when a large group of people come together, do the same thing, experience deep emotions, and find unity in a group. Some scholars have deemed these important for wellbeing and see them as a way of elevating the mundane to the sacred. Compare, for example, listening to pop punk band Blink-182 at home versus being at their concert and singing along with thousands of people.[39] Human play can happen at large social scales with elevating effects. But it can also happen in smaller places, where we enjoy the intrinsic pleasures of conversations, jokes, and fantastical stories. Some of these places are termed "third places" by sociologists, who distinguish them from our first-place homes and second-place job sites. These places enable us to experience leisure together. And some sociologists judge them crucial to human civilization.[40] Take the leisure space of taverns, for example. In 18th-century New York, John Hughson's taverns provided a rare space where white and black people could interact, long before the Emancipation Proclamation or Civil Rights Era. Taverns in the American Colonies became places where people could entertain ideas from many disciplines and cultures, eventually fomenting revolution. Additionally, in 1960s Los Angeles, spaces like Black Cat Tavern provided a place for gay people to enjoy themselves openly. Leisure and play combined in public spaces not only to transgress boundaries but also to challenge social and political restrictions on the way society organized itself, as well as to create new ways of being fuller humans and relating to others more genuinely and fully. These were far from idealistic spaces, however. Hughson was prosecuted for crimes that happened in and around his tavern. Some historians speculate that he was prosecuted harshly precisely because he provided a space where different races could mix. The Black Cat Tavern was also the site of an infamous incident where the Los Angeles Police Department beat and hospitalized several gay men for their "lewdness."[41] Play sometimes has serious consequences, and its effects reach beyond the activities.

The games themselves can also break barriers. American football was developed largely through the work of Native American students at Carlisle Academy under their coach Pop Warner, who began working with the team in 1899. They challenged the game's rules by inventing plays so that they could beat the larger, faster, and more prominent teams of universities like Yale. The students took the game of football beyond bone-breaking scrums to the complex formations and advanced strategies in the game today.[42] Similarly, baseball became an arena where race relations in the United States were challenged. Jackie Robinson's entry into a segregated baseball league in 1947 was a victory not only for baseball but also for wider social movements that were protesting the segregation in the American legal system, workforce, and housing market.[43] Ice hockey has a similar story too.[44] These historical examples show that human play and games are more complicated than anything in the non-human world. Even when playing games, the stakes, in many ways, are much higher than mere biological survival; play can impact identity and dignity, and it can imagine and create new possibilities for being human. These added normative elements transform how humans interact with each other and the values that they pass on.

Philosopher Cynthia Willett cherishes play so much that she argues that it can become a basis for an interspecies ethic. That is, through play, we can learn values that not only guide individual humans but also humans in their interactions with each other and other species. Building on the work of biologist Marc Bekoff, she identifies four central features of play. First, play involves role-reversals, as when large animals play with small animals and let them win. Second, play involves self-handicapping, as when large animals hold back their strength when playing with weaker animals.

Third, animals that play frequently communicate with each other, such as dogs when play-bowing with each other. This gesture ensures that play does not turn into fighting or mating. Fourth, play spreads a positive mood. Two animals may begin playing, but eventually more join in if allowed. Willett's analysis of play shows that play embodies equality, non-hierarchical relations, and open communication with others. While she admits that play can be a source of cruelty, she hopes that these features can also be a source of joy. And in the human world, play can be used to undermine oppressive hierarchies, reinforce equal standing, and enrich relationships. Moreover, she argues that play can connect humans to non-humans in a fundamental way that individualistic, anthropocentric Western ethics might not.[45] Even though she would not like this characterization, for me, the most important part of her research is that it shows how profoundly different human play is from non-human play. Play, in humans, goes beyond individual behavior or social coordination; it becomes a basis for understanding and manipulating abstract values and ideas and how we codify them in communities and institutions. In humans, play displays the four features that Willett identifies to a more idealized and profound extent.

Human Play

Here we are, with a cacophony of claims. How can we harmonize them? I think that the research shows that nearly all humans value play. Social psychologist Shalom Schwartz surveyed people on every inhabited continent, and he identified play as something valued in every culture. It was nested in a value he called "stimulation," or the desire for excitement, novelty, and challenges that people can meet.[46] What this means is that theorizing about play and pleasure transcends idiosyncrasy and applies to most of the human species.

Economists and political scientists conducted similar research. They examined humans across cultures to see whether there was a list of capacities that all humans have that governments should protect and cultivate. Instead of focusing on individual liberties, legal enforcement, or economic maximization, theorists like Amartya Sen began to ask what it takes to live a good life as a human. This led philosopher Martha Nussbaum to develop her capabilities approach to human rights, which lists ten capabilities as essential for human flourishing. She concluded that play is one of them, and therefore, that play is an indicator of human rights and development. According to her, citizens ought to be afforded opportunities to laugh and enjoy recreation. Such opportunities partially constitute a good human life. Or, stated otherwise, a life lacking play lacks something crucial for flourishing and justice.[47]

Nussbaum emphasizes that play, like all items on her list of central human capabilities, is ordered by practical reason and affiliation. This means that people must be able to think about and pursue what it means to live well and what is choiceworthy in life, and they must also be able to associate with people as citizens, peers, and friends. Without practical reason and affiliation, basic capacities turn into mere animal instincts. By emphasizing practical reason and affiliation, she ensures that a human level of care is afforded for even basic capacities. Take something like the need to eat. Someone can throw slop at a person to help him survive. But that is not sufficient for a good life based on the Aristotelian view or capabilities approach. When *people* eat, they spice and decorate food; they put their culture into dishes. My mother will cook you sopapillas and enchiladas, not just hand you piles of corn and meat. When people eat, they eat with one another to share sustenance and company; they nourish not only their bodies but also their souls and relationships. My mother will invite you to our table, and my father will discuss with you the lack of rain or the Raiders' latest (usually disappointing) football season.[48] People eat food with one another. They do not inhale nutrients in isolation. This considered social attention that people pay to activities is what makes the activities truly human. The same goes for play. Just giving someone a ball to play with is not enough. Rather, on Nussbaum's theory, a government must also make sure that people have opportunities to exercise their reason and social capacities in play. Play should be something that people can choose to do and express their reasoning through, and it should be something that allows them to connect with others. Play cannot be a mere animal exercise; it must be an opportunity suffused with thinking and complex sociality.[49]

Biologists and psychologists think that play can go wrong too. Over the past hundred years, IQs have risen steadily, a phenomenon dubbed the "Flynn Effect" after the psychologist who noticed the trend.[50] But anxiety, depression, feelings of helplessness, narcissism, and suicide are also on the rise. Part of this can be explained by the correlation between intelligence, creativity, and mental disorders.[51] Relative intelligence and creativity are positively correlated with depression, anxiety, bipolar disorder, and schizotypal qualities. So, it makes sense that, if groups of us are getting smarter, and if the observed trend holds, then it is likely that smarter groups of us will also be prone to psychological challenges. But other scientists—such as Sergio Pellis, Peter Gray, and Stuart Brown—have pointed to another cause for declining mental health in the developed world.[52] They lament childhood's lack of appropriately open, risky, and unsupervised play. Today, schools allow less time for children to play at recess and exclude many activities, sports, and games due to concerns for safety and legal liability. Additionally, helicopter parents prevent their children from playing in the wilderness, learning to use dangerous tools, or roughhousing with each other. As a result, these scientists say, this prevents children from developing the emotional skills that they need to regulate stress, cope with unpredictability, and adapt to an environment that does not yield to them in every way. This does not mean that children should be left alone in a macho, anarcho-primitivist hellscape like *Lord of the Flies*.[53] But the youngest generation suffers from parents isolating their children from all risks and safe opportunities to experience failure.[54] And this seems to adversely affect mental health and the psychological skills that play used to develop in childhood. Additionally, it does not seem that current popular methods of play—such as television, video games, and socializing through social media—provide the same benefits.[55] This is not alarmism about technology and the newest generation; rather, it is an observation that if childhood and play change, then the type of adult that gets raised will also likely change.[56]

What is worse, differences in play behavior sometimes separate by gender and produce disparate ill effects. Reshma Saujani links childhood activities to adult accomplishments. However, she argues that girls face a dearth of opportunities to fail and train courage, whereas boys often engage in risky play and become comfortable with failure. This difference in play and development means that girls are encouraged to play it safe. This has wide-ranging effects on the careers that women explore and the traits that they develop. Women, she argues, are hindered by a sense of perfection and aversion to failure. Saujani therefore argues that part of women's struggles for equality should include teaching girls to take chances, embrace failure, and move forward.[57] The games we play influence not only who we become but who we even *imagine* becoming.

So where does this leave us? I think that the work of scientists shows us that play helps animals to develop their neuromuscular and psychosocial systems, and it helps them to gain knowledge of themselves, their environment, and their kin. I also think that the social sciences and humanities show that humans uniquely play with values—as in transgressing taboos surrounding vulgar or deviant behaviors, experimenting with social values in a stratified society, and manipulating the norms used for identity and social coordination. This, to me, confirms the political conclusion that play is a profound feature of all human life, such that people suffer an injustice if afforded no opportunity to play. And this play should engage all of the capacities that humans have, but it should also (sometimes and under the right circumstances) involve appropriate risk and challenge to allow the players to develop stress responses, coping skills, and novel skillsets. This list of theses harmonizes the cacophonous claims that scholars have made about play. Because play is inextricable from human development and leading a good life, authors ascribe extraordinary properties to it. It makes sense why Huizinga and others find play at the root of human life, why he sees humans as *sub specie ludi*, viewed under and through the lens of play. However, this list of theses also shows the plurality and disjointedness of different aspects of play. This makes sense of comments critical of play, as in Plato. Critics are worried about the ways that play, especially for humans, can stunt existential, moral, and political progress by interacting with identity, values, and social coordination in the wrong ways.

Aristotle also thought play was complicated. And in fact, complication is a part of virtues and vices. For example, courage, the virtue helping us to regulate fear, is distinguished from vices that mimic courage, such as the civic 'courage' of people who act courageously to avoid dishonor and the martial 'courage' of people who act courageously because they are commanded to by a powerful officer (*EN* III.3-9). A multi-faceted behavior like play mirrors the complexity of Aristotle's traditional virtues. Some instances seem good, others bad. Play mirrors the complexity of human life itself because it is involved in many fundamental aspects of human functioning. And such a physically, psychologically, and socially complex phenomenon makes it probable that a virtue lies nearby. If playfulness is a virtue, it makes sense that it would follow the many complicated patterns of other virtues in Aristotle's system. The challenge then is to integrate the data about play as an action, as expressed here by scientists and humanists, into an ethical theory that is sensitive to the complexities of human psychology and behavior. In the next chapter, I will argue that playfulness as a virtue (as well as its corresponding vices) provides such a framework that can organize the disparate claims about play.

Notes

1 Gordon Burghardt, *The Genesis of Animal Play: Testing the Limits* (Cambridge, MA: The MIT Press, 2006), p. 405.
2 I am more interested in evaluating play than defining it. However, a few definitions deserve mentioning. Bernard Suits has probably the most famous: "x is playing if and only if x has made a temporary reallocation to autotelic activities of resources primarily committed to instrumental purposes." "Words on Play," *Journal of the Philosophy of Sport*, Appendix I: Presidential Address, vol. 4, no. 1 (1977): p. 124. Michael Ridge also provides a clear definition: "An agent is playing just in case the agent is engaged in unscripted activity for the fun of it." "Why So Serious? The Nature and Value of Play," *Philosophy and Phenomenological Research*, vol. 105 (2022): pp. 412. Scott Eberle also defines play: "Play is an ancient, voluntary, 'emergent' process driven by pleasure that yet strengthens our muscles, instructs our social skills, tempers and deepens our positive emotions, and enables a state of balance that leaves us poised to play some more." "The Elements of Play: Toward a Philosophy and a Definition of Play," *Journal of Play*, vol. 6, no. 2 (2014): p. 231. Biologists also define play because they need both careful criteria to distinguish playful from non-playful behavior and stopgaps against anthropomorphizing the animals they observe. Gordon Burghardt offers a famous biological definition: "Play is repeated, incompletely functional behavior differing from more serious versions structurally, contextually, or ontogenetically, and initiated voluntarily when the animal

is in a relaxed or low-stress setting." *Genesis*, p. 82. See also: Emily Ryall, "Playing with Words: Further Comment on Suits' Definition" in: *The Philosophy of Play*, ed. Emily Ryall, Wendy Russell, and Malcolm MacLean (London: Routledge, 2014), ch. 3; Thomas Hurka, "Games and the Good," *Proceedings of the Aristotelian Society*, suppl. vol., vol. 80 (2006): pp. 217–35 (as well as John Tasioulas' response, pp. 237–64.).
3 Moritz Schlick, "On the Meaning of Life," trans. Peter Heath, in: *Philosophical Papers*, vol. II [1925–1936], ed. H. Mulder and Barbara F. B. van de Velde-Schlick (Dordrecht, Holland: D. Reidel Publishing Company, 1979), p. 115.
4 Miguel Sicart, *Play Matters* (Cambridge, MA: The MIT Press, 2014), p. 1.
5 "You Can Discover More About a Person in an Hour of Play than in a Year of Conversation: Plato? Richard Lingard? Anonymous?" *Quote Investigator*, (30 July 2015): https://quoteinvestigator.com/2015/07/30/hour-play/.
6 For a different survey of claims about play, see: Randolph Feezell, "A Pluralistic Conception of Play" in *The Philosophy of Play*, ed. Ryall, Russell, and MacLean, ch. 1. Feezell includes quotes by Colin McGinn, such as,

Play is a vital part of any full life, and a person who never plays is worse than a 'dull boy': he or she lacks imagination, humour and a proper sense of value. Only the bleakest and most life-denying Puritanism could warrant deleting all play from human life. ... Play is a part of what makes human life worthwhile, and we should seek to get as much out of it as we can.

Feezell also includes poet Diane Ackerman, who writes,

The spirit of deep play is central to the life of each person, and also to society, inspiring the visual, musical, and verbal arts; exploration and discovery; war; law; and other elements of culture we have come to cherish (or dread).

Lastly, Feezell includes the claims of neuroscientist Stuart Brown, who writes,

I don't think it is too much to say that play can save your life. It certainly has salvaged mine. Life without play is a grinding, mechanical existence organized around doing things necessary for survival. Play is the stick that stirs the drink. It is the basis of all art, games, books, sports, movies, fashion, fun, and wonder—in short, the basis of what we think of as civilization. Play is the vital essence of life.

(Pp. 13–4)

7 Johan Huizinga, *Homo Ludens: A Study of the Play-Element in Culture* (Kettering, OH: Angelic Press, 2016), p. 5. The title of the book incorporates into the species name for humans the Latin word for "play." In fact, he wants to see human culture as "*sub specie ludi*" instead of *sub specie aeternitatis*.
8 Steven Johnson, *Wonderland: How Play Made the Modern World* (New York: Riverhead Books, 2016), p. 12.
9 John Wall, "All the World's a Stage: Childhood and the Play of Being" in: *The Philosophy of Play*, ed. Ryall, Russell, and MacLean, pp. 34–9. Wall finds fault with all three camps. Top-down thinkers are too harsh, and they understate the importance of play for creativity, innovation, and motivation of action. Bottom-up thinkers sentimentalize children and ignore the ways in which they struggle with identity formation and social belonging, none of which are placid or given in childhood experience. Developmental thinkers get the spectrum of development right, evaluating children and adults on a gradient, but they also minimize the qualitative break between childhood and adulthood, as well as the fact that the sophisticated norms of adulthood are what evaluate children and development.

10 Though omitted for space, Plato's *Laws*, Roland Barthes' *S/Z*, Hans Georg-Gadamer's *Truth and Method*, Mikhail Bakhtin's *Rabelais and His World*, and Donald Winnicott's *Playing and Reality* could all be added.
11 I largely pull evidence from mammals that play, especially rats, dolphins, and primates. Mammals are less mysterious to biologists than other taxonomic classes. However, evidence suggests that non-mammals also play, for example, birds, reptiles, fish, and invertebrates. Here, though, biologists struggle with interpreting playful behavior without anthropomorphizing, as well as explaining whether playful behavior evolved once in a primal ancestor or many times over the course of history. See: Burghardt, *Genesis*, chs. 11–14.
12 For the biology of play, see: Burghardt, *Genesis*; Patrick Bateson and Paul Martin, *Play, Playfulness, Creativity, and Innovation* (Cambridge: Cambridge University Press, 2013).
13 Bateson and Martin, *Play*, p. 35.
14 Two examples of social learning via play: (1) Galapagos woodpecker finches have dispositions to pick up sticks, but they learn from others to put sticks into holes to find insect larvae. (2) Bottlenose dolphins in Shark Bay, Australia, put basket sponges on their beaks to scour the sea floor for prey, a skill passed on from mother to daughter. Bateson and Martin, *Play*, pp. 51–2, 73–4.
15 Bateson and Martin, *Play*, pp. 14, 23, 29–33, 123.
16 Sergio and Vivien Pellis emphasize that "play fighting" does not resemble "serious fighting" in rats. In play, rats nuzzle each other's necks, while in combat, rats bite each other's hinds. The responses are different too. In play, rats are distressed when their partners do not reciprocate the nuzzles or defend against them. While play involves some competition, it also requires cooperation because the play cannot proceed without both rats playing along. Additionally, rats are less likely to play with each other if one rat constantly wins. Both rats must be willing to switch roles and give the other a fair shot at nuzzling or getting nuzzled. "Play fighting" may therefore be used as shorthand, but it is technically questionable. *The Playful Brain: Venturing to the Limits of Neuroscience* (Oxford: Oneworld, 2009), pp. 15–25, 42–3.
17 Pellis and Pellis, *Playful Brain*, pp. 46–54. Decorticated rats do play differently than rats with the whole brain. But they will still exhibit playful behavior and try to play with others in contests that result in a 50/50 win-loss ratio.
18 Pellis and Pellis, *Playful Brain*, pp. 63, 72–4, 189 n. 78.
19 Bateson and Martin, *Play*, p. 37.
20 Pellis and Pellis, *Playful Brain*, ch. 5.
21 Pellis and Pellis, *Playful Brain*, ch. 4, esp. pp. 86–7. The Pellises temper their conclusion, suggesting that the play-enriched rats might discover new ways of responding to predators. For example, running under cover might work for most predators (like cats). But against owls, rats survive better if they run directly at the owls. The playful rats were more likely to discover these novel strategies for survival than those that stuck to the conventional patterns of behavior, but this comes at the costs mentioned above. For the most relevant experiments, see: p. 188 n. 68; esp. Aileen D. Gruendel and William J. Arnold, "Influence of Preadolescent Experiential Factors on the Development of Sexual Behavior in Albino Rats," *Journal of Comparative and Physiological Psychology*, vol. 86, no. 1 (1974): pp. 172–8.
22 The argument also extends beyond playfighting to types of play between mothers and their offspring and the playful activities surrounding grooming. Pellis and Pellis, *Playful Brain*, pp. 62–5, 100–1, 122–9.
23 Bateson and Martin, *Play*, pp. 4–5, 72–4.

24 This seems speculative on the part of biologists. To me, it is unclear whether the bubble-blowing play behavior developed first or whether the bubble-based hunting methods developed first and then were adapted to play. The way to test this would be to see if animals do one without the other. But I have found no such source.
25 Bateson and Martin, *Play*, pp. 30–1.
26 Bateson and Martin, *Play*, pp. 19–23.
27 Biologists have noted that playful activity often correlates with large brains relative to body size, and humans have this feature. Pellis and Pellis, *Playful Brain*, pp. 55, 130–2. For neoteny in humans, see: Stuart Brown, "Play is more than fun," *TED Talk: 2008 Art Center Design Conference—Serious Play*, Pasadena, CA, May 2008. Published on YouTube (12 March 2009).
28 Plato makes a similar point, writing

> I insist that a man who intends to be good at a particular occupation must practice it from childhood: both at work and at play he must be surrounded by special 'tools of the trade.' For instance, the man who intends to be a good farmer must play at farming, and the man who is to be a good builder must spend his playtime building toy houses; and in each case the teacher must provide miniature tools that copy the real thing. ... To sum up, we say that the correct way to bring up and educate a child is to use his playtime to imbue his soul with the greatest possible liking for the occupation in which he will have to be absolutely perfect when he grows up.
>
> *Laws*, trans. Trevory J. Saunders in: *Plato: Complete Works*, ed. John M. Cooper, assc. ed. D. S. Hutchinson (Indianapolis: Hackett, 1997), 643b-d

29 See: Walter Sinnott-Armstrong, ed., *Moral Psychology: Volume 3: The Neuroscience of Morality: Emotion, Brain Disorders and Development* (Cambridge, MA: The MIT Press, 2008); Tommaso Bruni, Matteo Mameli, and Regina A. Rini, "The Science of Morality and Its Normative Implications," *Neuroethics*, vol. 7 (2014): pp. 159–72.
30 Cynthia Willett, *Interspecies Ethics* (New York: Columbia University Press), p. 75–6; Bateson and Martin, *Play*, p. 17.
31 On equifinality, see: Martin and Bateson, *Play*, p. 34. The lesson on humbling what play can do uniquely, I owe to my dissertation committee members: John Lachs, Jeffrey Tlumak, Kelly Oliver, Robert B. Talisse, and Christian B. Miller.
32 Bateson and Martin, *Play*, p. 30. Monkeys may fling poo, and dogs may pee on each other. But neither activity is being played with. Bodily functions may be a means to assert dominance without being the subject of play.
33 People writing their names in snow with urine, pranks involving poop, and mullet contests refute critics who question that we make games of urinating, defecating, or grooming.
34 See: Alison Gopnik, *The Philosophical Baby: What Children's Minds Tell Us About Truth, Love, and the Meaning of Life* (New York: Farrar, Straus, and Giroux, 2009), pp. 70–3, 88–90, 228–9. While animals in some sense pretend, as in the case of chimpanzees caring for sticks, no animal seems to play with advanced rules or complex social roles as humans do.
35 See: Clifford Geertz, "Deep Play: Notes on the Balinese Cockfight," *Daedalus*, vol. 101, no. 1 (1972): pp. 27–9.
36 Linking non-human play to the evolution of morality, see: Marc Bekoff, "Social Play Behavior: Cooperation, Fairness, Trust, and the Evolution of Morality," *Journal of Consciousness Studies*, vol. 8, no. 2 (2001): pp. 81–90. For analyses of carnivals and jesters, see: Mikhail Bakhtin, *Rabelais and His World*, trans.

60 *Harmonizing the Cacophony of Claims about Play*

Helene Isolsky (Bloomington: Indiana University Press, 1984); Beatrice K. Otto, *Fools Are Everywhere: The Court Jester around the World* (Chicago: University of Chicago Press, 2007).

37 Johann Wolfgang von Goethe, "Geschichte Gottfriedens von Berlichingen mit der eisernen Hand," *Spiegel Online*, ch. 4, http://gutenberg.spiegel.de/buch/geschichte-gottfriedens-von-berlichingen-mit-der-eisernen-hand-3621/4. My translation. Here, I am also trying to follow E. B. White's advice not to explain why this is funny or what values it transgresses. He observed, "Explaining a joke is like dissecting a frog. You understand it better but the frog dies in the process."

38 Bateson and Martin, *Play*, p. 14 and ch. 9.

39 Collective effervescence is first described by Émile Durkheim in *The Elementary Forms of Religious Life*, which he used to distinguish the sacred from mundane. Scholars today, however, apply collective effervescence to mundane activities too. See: Shira Gabriel, Esha Naidu, *et al.*, "Creating the Sacred from the Profane: Collective Effervescence and Everyday Activities," *The Journal of Positive Psychology*, vol. 15, no. 1 (2020): pp. 129–54.

40 See: Ray Oldenberg, *The Great Good Place: Cafés, Coffee Shops, Bookstores, Bars, Hair Salons, and Other Hangouts at the Heart of a Community* (Boston: Marlowe & Company, 1999).

41 Steven Johnson, *Wonderland*, ch. 6.

42 Sally Jenkins, *The Real All Americans* (New York: Broadway Books, 2007).

43 Peter Dreier, "The Real Story of Baseball's Integration that You Won't See in *42*," *The Atlantic* (11 April 2013): https://www.theatlantic.com/entertainment/archive/2013/04/the-real-story-of-baseballs-integration-that-you-wont-see-in-i-42-i/274886/.

44 George Fosty and Darril Fosty, *Black Ice: The Lost History of the Colored Hockey League of the Maritimes, 1895–1925* (New York: Stryker-Indigo, 2004).

45 Willett, *Interspecies*, pp. 68, 75–9.

46 Schwartz used copious cross-cultural surveys and research projects to draw his conclusions. Shalom H. Schwartz, "Are There Universal Aspects in the Structure and Contents of Human Values?" *Journal of Social Issues*, vol. 50, no. 4 (1994): pp. 19–45. Other behavioral scientists also found play as a prevalent value in cross-cultural studies, for example: Frank W. Wicker, Frank B. Lambert, Frank C. Richardson, and Joseph Kahler, "Categorical Goal Hierarchies and Classification of Human Motives," *Journal of Personality*, vol. 52, no. 3 (Sept 1984): pp. 285–305. Through surveying dozens of cultures on every inhabited continent, Schwartz found a consistent human value for play. Moreover, Schwartz's survey method not only allowed him to find that all cultures valued stimulation, but he also found that stimulation had a positive correlation with other values, such as "hedonism" (experiencing pleasure for oneself). He also found a negative correlation between an openness to change (the umbrella category for stimulation and hedonism) and conservativeness (of which values like conformity and security are parts).

47 Martha C. Nussbaum, *Women and Human Development: The Capabilities Approach* (Cambridge: Cambridge University Press, 2000), pp. 78–80. Her complete list of capabilities is: sustaining life; cultivating bodily health; maintaining bodily integrity; using senses, imagination, and thought; feeling emotions; engaging in practical reason; enjoying affiliations; interacting with other species; playing; and controlling aspects of one's environment.

48 My father died during the time it took me to revise this manuscript. *Descanse en paz.*

49 Nussbaum, *Women and Human Development*, pp. 77–83. See also: Martha Nussbaum, "Nature, Function, and Capability: Aristotle on Political Distribution,"

Oxford Studies in Ancient Philosophy, suppl. vol. I (1988): pp. 145–84; "Aristotelian Social Democracy" in: *Liberalism and the Good*, ed. R. Bruce Douglass, Gerald M. Mara, and Henry S. Richardson (New York: Routledge, 1990), ch. 10; "Aristotle on Human Nature and the Foundations of Ethics" in: *World, Mind, and Ethics: Essays on the Ethical Philosophy of Bernard Williams*, eds. J. E. J. Altham and Ross Harrison (Cambridge: Cambridge UP, 1995), ch. 6. For a detailed Marxian discussion of human activity and sociality, see: Daniel Brudney, "Community and Completion" in: *Reclaiming the History of Ethics: Essays for John Rawls*, eds. Andrews Reath, Barbara Herman, and Christine M. Korsgaard (Cambridge: Cambridge UP, 1997), pp. 388–415.

50 For a discussion of the Flynn Effect, see: David Shenk, "What is the Flynn Effect, and How Does It Change Our Understanding of IQ?" *WIREs Cognitive Science*, vol. 8 (Jan-Apr 2019). Some recent evidence suggests that the nutritional, developmental, and economic drivers behind the Flynn Effect have finally plateaued.

51 Bateson and Martin, *Play*, pp. 62–4. See also: Pellis and Pellis, *The Playful Brain*, chs. 7–8.

52 Mental health and human wellbeing are complex. None of the scientists would say that play deprivation is the *sole* cause for declining mental health. But they would point to it as a major cause.

53 Heeding the advice of scientists lamenting the loss of risky play, Wildwood Forest Schools have been opening all over Europe and some in the United States. These schools are designed to teach children to light fires, use knives, forage for food, and play in the outdoors. The founders cite increased self-confidence, autonomy, and freedom as their primary concerns for children who go through their schools. See: Jo Tweedy, "Inside the Scandinavian-style Forest Schools Where Parents Pay for Children to Learn How to Get Dirty, Play with Knives and Light Fires," *Daily Mail* (10 Nov 2015): http://www.dailymail.co.uk/femail/article-3302171/Inside-Scandinavian-style-forest-schools-parents-PAY-children-learn-dirty-play-knives-light-fires.html; and Alice Gregory, "Running Free in Germany's Outdoor Preschools," *The New York Times Style Magazine* (18 May 2017): https://www.nytimes.com/2017/05/18/t-magazine/germany-forest-kindergarten-outdoor-preschool-waldkitas.html.

54 See: Steven Horwitz, *Hayek's Modern Family* (New York: Palgrave Macmillan, 2015), ch. 8; Peter Gray, *Free to Learn: Why Unleashing the Instinct to Play Will Make Our Children Happier, More Self-Reliant, and Better Students of Life* (New York: Basic Books, 2013). More needs said to establish causation instead of correlation, however.

55 The effects of social media and technology on wellbeing are complicated. Social media seems to exacerbate depression and anxiety, lead to sleep deprivation, deteriorate body image, present risks for cyberbullying, and create a fear of missing out. But it also offers an opportunity for people to read about mental health and learn from people's experiences. Social media might also build supportive communities and aid in identity formation. Royal Society for Public Health, *#StatusOfMind: Social Media and Young People's Mental Health and Wellbeing* (19 May 2017): https://www.rsph.org.uk/about-us/news/instagram-ranked-worst-for-young-people-s-mental-health.html; Nadine Mulfinger, Sabine Müller, et al., "Honest, Open, Proud for Adolescents with Mental Illness: Pilot Randomized Controlled Trial," *Journal of Child Psychology and Psychiatry*, vol. 59, no. 6 (05 Dec 2017); Jean M. Twenge, Thomas E. Joiner, Megan L. Rogers, and Gabrielle N. Martin, "Increases in Depressive Symptoms, Suicide-Related Outcomes, and Suicide Rates Among U.S. Adolescents After 2010 and Links to Increased New Media Screen Time," *Association for*

Psychological Science: Clinical Psychological Science, vol. 6, no. 1 (2018): pp. 3–17. Also consider political uses of social media, such as those involved in *The Arab Spring* and the *January 6th United States Capitol Attack*.
56 Bateson and Martin, *Play*, pp. 98–102.
57 See: Reshma Saujani, *Brave, Not Perfect: Fear Less, Fail More, and Live Bolder* (New York: Penguin, 2019).

4 The Virtue of Playfulness

Most animals cannot live well without playing. In fact, play is so important that it can serve as a marker of wellbeing. This is because play provides both positive and negative indications. Stressed animals do not play, and play teaches valuable lessons. For example, play teaches rats how to cope with the anxiety of unpredictable environments and actors. So, play-deprived rats cannot coordinate their bodies with non-stationary objects, and they become stressed in uncertain situations. This means that play-deprived rats can neither mount potential mates nor make friends. Another case is dolphins. Some teach each other skills while playing, for example, to use sponges to scrape the sea floor for food.[1] Play-deprived dolphins, therefore, would lose out on skills for optimal survival, as well as social connections. Play can impact almost every aspect of life. For individual animals, the complex maneuvers of play train their neuromuscular systems and psychological resilience to stress. For groups of animals, the social interactions that occur during play create bonds and transmit skills. During play, animals hone their bodies, test their minds, familiarize themselves with their kin, and interact with other species and the wider environment. Simply, play prepares animals for life.

The stakes are even higher for humans, and the point holds across age groups. Beginning around age five, children mimic and manipulate rules, values, and social roles in the games that they play.[2] This sets the stage for adopting social roles and coordinating group behavior. Games, rituals, and art transform larval toddlers into adolescents and adults who understand the abstract world of value and the complex dynamics of social interactions. But play is also important for adults who already understand these things. Play helps adults rest from work and stimulate themselves after drudgery, a trend found on every inhabitable continent in numerous cross-cultural surveys.[3] More poignant, play deprivation breaks people, and these broken people make broken communities. Psychologist Stuart Brown studied dozens of murderers at the infamous prison in Huntsville, Texas. In the prisoners' lives, he consistently found childhood play deprivation. This was especially obvious in the case of Charles Whitman, the

DOI: 10.4324/9781032717722-5

sniper who killed 17 people at the University of Texas.[4] Play maintains psychological health in the face of toil and obligations. And people without play cannot work well, much less live well or create just communities. The *action of play* is undoubtedly necessary for a good life.

However, despite these observations about play, thinkers quarrel endlessly about it. For example, Plato, in *Republic*, warns against improper play and the ways it can deform the soul. Whereas Jean-Jacques Rousseau, in *Emile*, deems play a pearl of authentic goodness to be preserved from childhood onward. Philosophers disagree about which types of play are good or bad, as well as just how good or bad they are. Rats run, fish swim, philosophers disagree, fine. But usually, philosophers understand where the disagreements are. And that is what is so disconcerting about play. Especially with this topic, philosophers seem to talk past each other.

The standard philosophical strategy is to argue about the definition of "play" and the propriety of the *action* of play. Many excellent scholars have done and continue to do this work.[5] However, I want to take a different route. In this chapter, I argue that a *character trait of playfulness* can help us to make sense of the disparate claims about play. I hope that my theory of playfulness can do two things: (1) organize the plurality of claims about play by using a framework of virtues and vices and (2) defend playfulness as indispensable to a good life. My description of playfulness should show why some philosophers deride play but others revere it. It should also sketch a trait that can guide our actions and ethical reflections on play and living well. While my characterization will not produce a list of necessary and sufficient conditions, it should be enough to distinguish play from non-play and good play from bad play. My goal here is not to set strict semantic limits but rather to propose some practical boundaries, even if occasionally porous. And I invite other philosophers to contribute to this ongoing debate.

My characterization will hinge on one curiosity about humans: we face leisure time explicitly. We ask each other things like, "What are you doing this weekend?" or "What kind of things are you into when not working?" And we can use our practical reason and complex sociality during free time, as in playing games or organizing parties. Using our capacities well during leisure, I argue, is being playful. In other words, we have time that we do not need to spend on mere survival, so we face choices about how to use our leisure. It is here that the virtue of playfulness helps. *Playfulness helps us to use our leisure time well by resting, developing ourselves, and engaging our communities via intrinsically valued activities that lead us toward better lives.* And without playfulness, we neglect creativity, innovation, and inquiry into the values that we assume in our individual and communal lives.

A quick stylistic note: I generally use feminine pronouns for the virtuous person and masculine ones for vicious person as a way to clarify the back-and-forth discussion between virtues and vices.

Leisure Time as the Sphere of Playfulness

The goal of life is to be happy. Aristotle thinks that we stand the best chance of accomplishing happiness by becoming as good of people as possible by developing virtues and avoiding vices. For Aristotle, the virtues are the moral character traits that help us regulate emotions or spheres of life that all humans face. And each virtue regulates a unique sphere within the Aristotelian system. Cumulatively, the virtues therefore add up to a set of moral character traits that we need to develop in order to live well. Each virtue helps us to face a different aspect of life in the best way possible.

Whether or not we want to, we repeatedly interact with the many spheres of life. These interactions mean that we cannot avoid forming dispositions in relation to them. Life happens. We react. Life happens in the same way again. We react in the same way again. And eventually, we develop a disposition toward a specific aspect of life. The Aristotelian hope is that we learn to take control of this process so that the dispositions that we do develop are the ones that can help us to flourish.[6] For example, we cannot help but face fear, so we develop courage, cowardice, or foolhardiness over a lifetime. Or, when pleasures present themselves, we become temperate, indulgent, or ascetic through our responses.

It is important to emphasize here that it would be a bad idea to let our dispositions form on their own, automatically and unreflectively (*EN* 1099b24). Part of being human means that we can think about why we do what we do and how we accomplish what we aim to do. This is called *practical reason*, and it is central to Aristotle's ethical system. Additionally, humans are social animals, so we have the opportunity to talk with others, thus making our actions comprehensible to our friends, mentors, and community members, who then can offer advice or coordinate with us. This is the *complex sociality* that humans exhibit in our interactions with one another. Both practical reason and sociality deeply impact the development of virtues and the ability to manage the competing goods of life on the way to happiness.

Some might ask: why care about forming good character? Aristotle replied to similar critics by noting that people literally destroy their own lives by exclusively pursuing wealth or manliness or whatever value they take to be most important in life, when in actuality, it was the wrong thing to go after (*EN* 1094b19-20).[7] The stakes of developing our characters are no more or no less than our happiness or misery. Malformed, vicious character endangers ethical life, but a carefully cultivated, virtuous character improves it. Someone who is an ascetic coward will be worse off than someone who developed temperance and courage. In other words, someone who enjoys life's pleasures and avoids debilitating fear lives better than someone who shuns pleasures and crumples under anxiety. Who we are matters for how we live.

So, for playfulness to be a virtue, there must be some situation or emotion that is universal to human life that playfulness regulates to make us happier. I propose that playfulness regulates our *leisure time*. By "leisure time," I mean the time that we have in spurts or stretches that is free from immediate concerns for somatic, psychological, social, or economic survival.[8] Leisure *time*, in my view, can include a range of *activities*. It can include rest, relaxation, recreation, or simply doing nothing.[9] It can include idleness or those activities that are low-effort, unconcerned with worldly affairs, and taken up simply for their sheer joy.[10] It can include play, especially the activities that are chosen for themselves and contain some degree of fun.[11] It can include more intense activities such as learning, creating art, playing a sport, or anything that might take a long-term, high-energy commitment.[12] Additionally, any and all of these activities can be directed primarily at ourselves or at our communities. We can strive for self-improvement or social engagement. I do not think that we need more than general characterizations here of each activity that I listed. Strict and uncontested definitions of leisure and its activities are difficult to come by.[13] Nonetheless, it would be disingenuous of me not to point out that many scholars connect leisure to the meaning and purpose of life.[14] Philosopher Sarah Broadie, I think, explains why. She connects the lack of necessity in leisure time, as well as the activities that we pursue during it, to our deepest values. She writes, "This was the quintessential fruit of leisure; it came into being not because it matched a requirement, but because it was a new thing to love."[15] Leisure is born of freedom and reveals our love. And how we live our freedom and choose our loves reflects the deepest values that we hold.

Leisure's prominence and importance in human life beg its confrontation. Aristotle argued that leisure is necessary for both people and communities to flourish, "And happiness is thought to depend on leisure; for we are busy that we may have leisure and make war that we may live in peace" (*EN* 1177b5-6). We show ourselves worthy of freedom when we use our free time well, and inversely, we show ourselves debased whenever we pursue nothing but useful or practical things (*Pol.* 1338b2-4). This point holds not only for individuals but for entire states too. Remember Aristotle's remarks on the Spartans and imperialism. Communities and people who do not know how to be free end up destroying themselves (*Pol.* VII.14). This is why he advocated so strongly for a state-sponsored educational program. And this program connected times of peace and leisure to *gymnasion* and *mousikē*, athletic training and the arts of the Muses, or more colloquially and contemporarily, almost every kid's favorite times of the school day: physical education, recess, music, and art. The liberal arts—everything from play to philosophical theory—are parts of the education that all citizens need (*Pol.* VIII.3). This is because they teach us to be free; they teach us to be human. In Aristotle's works, play is usually near these conversations. Play contributes to childhood development, and play is a medicine to help adults through labor and drudgery (*EN* X.6-7; *Pol.* VII.17). Aristotle himself did not even consider playfulness as a candidate for being a virtue. But Aristotle did identify a sphere of life essential to flourishing for individuals and to justice for communities: leisure. And in those same conversations, he consistently referenced play and all activities related to the sphere of leisure, such as relaxation and rest. So, it seems right to pay special attention to leisure and its connections to play. It is puzzling that Aristotle himself said nothing about any virtue that may regulate such an important sphere as leisure and crucial activity as play, especially because both get mentioned in his most famous practical works, repeatedly. But such a crucial oversight is why I propose playfulness here as the virtue that regulates what we do in our leisure, play included among its activities.

Contemporary scholarship largely concurs with Aristotle's arguments that leisure is important. Scholars argue that leisure is a near-universal feature of human life today, even if only in small stints of time.[16] Leisure is accessible too. People can exert control over their leisure time more easily than controlling their economic power, social status, or physical health. People can enjoy leisure for free through activities like hiking, running, reading, and listening to music. Moreover, how people spend their leisure time dramatically affects how satisfied they feel with life. The more leisure time they have, the better they feel. The better they use it, the better they feel.[17] To me, all of this evidence adds up to a virtue existing with respect to leisure time. Moreover, because of leisure's prevalence, we cannot help but develop dispositions in relation to it. We all do something with that time, whether choosing to laze around or to fill our schedules with certification programs and competitive leagues. Even in smaller bits of time, we can choose between doomscrolling Facebook, shitposting on TikTok, running language exercises on Duolingo, or solving chess puzzles. This repeated exposure to spending our leisure time in certain ways leads to habit. Moreover, the habits surrounding our free time impact deep features of our personal characters and social lives. We often choose our friends based on common hobbies, and we discuss our hobbies frequently. Quality of life changes depending on the amount of leisure and its engagement.

Leisure activities serve many psychological purposes too. They often allow us to gain a sense of mastery within the activity, and these activities enrich our lives. Also, the activities usually become outlets for stress and emotions, and they help someone escape everyday worries. Leisure activities improve self-esteem and allow one to achieve focus and control in creative expression.[18] They entangle themselves in identity formation and self-fulfillment.[19]

Additionally, how we spend our leisure time and have fun reveals a lot about our psychological lives. Sometimes, we compensate for our non-leisurely lives. People with stressful careers sometimes need that fifth time streaming *Star Trek* from start to finish while they scroll through memes on the internet. But in that same regard, sometimes our leisure reveals our shortcomings as people. We may sense that we need to use leisure well, but under the guises of "harmless fun" or "just joking," we might also reveal our insensitivities to our own vices or to our own toxic effects on our communities. We could do this, for example, by only ever spending our leisure time binging Taco Bell and trolling people on the internet. Leisure has moral consequences for who we become, how we assess what we need, and how we form communities by interacting with those around us.

The celebration of leisure and play is not controversial in the abstract. The problem comes in considering *how* we should spend that time.[20] Not all leisure activities are equal. If we do not use our leisure time well, we do not live much better than people who lack leisure altogether. For example, many social scientists are skeptical of spending leisure time watching TV, as it seems to lack the benefits of active play. Children who only spend time watching TV or playing on iPads fare worse than children who play sports, tinker outdoors, or experience games with other children face-to-face.[21] Additionally, activities like dancing have much longer-lasting physical, psychological, and social benefits than watching TV. Dancers train their bodies, form communities, and immerse themselves in emotional music. All of these things elicit profound short-term and enduring long-term effects. TV watching, as prevalent and accessible as it is, might de-stress its viewers temporarily, but it does little by way of improving cardiovascular health, forming supportive communities, or evoking deep and long-lasting emotions.[22] Leisure activities have different benefits. And we must find a way to assess and compare activities.

After all, leisure activities have risks too. For example, extreme sports present high physical risks compared to others. BASE jumping—skydiving done by jumping off buildings, antennae, bridges, or cliffs—carries a fatality risk of roughly one in 60 participants.[23] But it also pushes the boundaries of human accomplishment, bringing thousands of dollars and viral popularity for the best athletes. By contrast, the habits of a nerd may be boring to some, but the risks of reading, watching movies, and socializing over meals are substantially less than those of riding motorcycles, bare-knuckle boxing, or doing designer drugs. Then again, the high is not quite the same either. This is not intended to strawman risky activities or shame nerds. Rather, I want to emphasize that different activities bear different disadvantages, and people must make these assessments themselves.

Complications multiply whenever we consider how politically transgressive leisure activities can be. To conservative communities, rock music worships the devil, coed dancing promotes loose morals, and drinking at a tavern with other races and queer folk indicates a character flaw. There are places in the world where people get beaten for drinking alcohol or much worse for non-marital relationships.[24] Spending leisure in play can be creative and egalitarian. And in communities that prefer hierarchies, play threatens social organization. Even in philosophy, both Plato and Aristotle warned against base forms of play because it can train children to have bad habits, and it can normalize perverse actions. These bad people, they worried, end up bad citizens.[25] There seems to be a communal stake in the ways that we use our leisure time, in how we play. George Santayana once remarked, "To the art of working well, a civilized race would add the art of playing well."[26]

There is also a much more contemporary concern about games and play. C. Thi Nguyen argues that games affect our very agency—our capacity for experiencing the world, interacting with values, and creating our own standards and life trajectories. Nguyen worries that repeated unreflective interaction with games can engrain in us harmful patterns of thought and being. For example, consider the ways games often have a singular and engrossing win condition, whereby players are invited to use everything and everyone to accomplish that end. Might engraining that particular skill in-game tempt players to use out-of-game all of their own values, goods, and projects (and the values, goods, and projects of others) as mere means to their end of winning the game of life? In other words, might people oversimplify life by thinking about it like a game? Could games instill the mindset of Bernie Madoff doing everything for money or Caesar vying for every shred of power? Nguyen is not worried much about violence in video games. He is more worried about games making us think that things outside of the game might also have such simple win conditions and such permissive rules to do anything to achieve them. Relatedly, he considers the clear metrics of games—the green bars that fill after gathering a resource, the health bar that decreases after damage, the statistical breakdown of a player's strength or charisma, or the end screen full of scores and statistics. Life is not so simple. We do not often know which values are operative at a given time in our lives or in a social space. We do not often know precisely how, for example, working an extra shift to earn more money will affect our health, family bonds, pursuit of hobbies, or political engagement. Games offer a fantasy of clear, commensurable, and rankable values. Maybe we see, then, the allure of striving after money like Madoff (or power like Caesar), which is easy to measure and manage. Nguyen worries that "… [W]e will be drawn to systems, institutions, social practices, and activities that closely resemble games, and we may be tempted to adjust our own goals to make our lives more closely resemble game-play."[27] The worry is that gamers may treat their own lives like the games that they play—not with violence and sex as conservative pundits panic about, but in a deep, unseen, and psychological way that makes us yearn for artificial clarity, quantifiability, and winnability in the face of life's complexity, vagueness, and sublimity. Athletes treat everything as sport, actors everything as performance, entertainers everything as a party, MBAs everything as an optimization of statistics. The same mind that we use for leisure is the same mind that we use for life. And the ways that we act and think in leisure should not always be applied to moral and political life. So maybe we should find some guidelines.

My question, then, is this: how can we assess leisure and all of the activities that we take up within it? Philosophy so far has been of little help, and no traditional virtue directly applies. I agree with Aristotle that we need leisure, and I agree with philosophers who argue that leisure and play have ethical stakes. I also realize that not all leisure activities are the same and vary widely with culture, interest, and demographics. But even in the face of the plurality of activities and choices, I think there is a solution: considering a virtue of playfulness.

Playfulness as a Virtue

Playfulness is the right way of responding to leisure time. In the virtue of playfulness, we get a character trait that can help distinguish good from bad play, no matter the variety of things that we do.[28] And we can reconcile the accounts of philosophers who deride and celebrate play. Just like any virtue, playfulness is psychologically complex. So, I must describe its components.

The Psychology of Playfulness

Cognitive Aspects

Playfulness has a large *cognitive component*. It involves understanding oneself and what one needs somatically, psychologically, and socially. A playful person will always ask: what is it that I most need from my leisure time? This takes self-awareness in the ability to assess oneself, and it takes practical reasoning in the ability to assess which goods, games, and experiences are both valuable and accessible to meet these demands. Humans require many things. And playful people use their leisure to rest, develop themselves, and engage their communities. Part of playfulness involves deciding to rest the parts of us that ache or rekindle the parts of us that have been snuffed out by travail. So, battered and dulled, we turn to our leisure, and we must select among the many things that we could do. Sometimes, I need a few hours of watching Jean-Luc Picard solve intergalactic problems. Sometimes, I need to catch up with friends and family on the phone. Other times, I need to challenge myself by running, lifting weights, or learning a new Polyphia song on guitar. The cognitive components of playfulness help me to balance the competing values of life and the goals that I have for my time. But how?

To make decisions about how to use our leisure, Aristotle uses *eudaimonia* to keep people focused on the holistic goal of living the best life humanly possible. Similarly, the playful person uses happiness to compare herself against. This enables her to see how best to move forward. Playfulness involves reflection during her free time to assess how she lives in the small moments and long buildups to life's goals. One thing is crucial: the playful person spends leisure with growth in mind.

People might object to my characterization of playfulness already, saying that it seems too cognitive and unfun. It feels as though there is a looming paradox, akin to the hedonic treadmill, where the more one strives to be playful, the further one gets from it.[29] After all, what is worse than someone trying hard to be playful or forcing others to have fun? Such a person usually deludes himself and annoys everyone else.

However, this is where Aristotle can help. Virtues are not just about the information that we consider, the principles in syllogisms, or the skillful know-how to do things. Yes, virtues involve this. But they also involve feelings, motivations, and the pursuit of full, effortless, sincere action. People who are not fully playful but working to cultivate playfulness may seem thought-heavy and clumsy, and they may grumble at assessing their free time and trying to find the best way to use it. But with more practice, it becomes easier. And people eventually feel better as they develop good habits, stay committed to leisure activities, and connect their free time to self-development. For Aristotelians, the goal of ethical action is never a mere set of actions or rules. Feelings and manner of execution matter too. People are not fully playful until they understand what needs to be done, feel good about doing it, stay motivated to do it, and sincerely act each time the virtue merits. So, if there is a ludic treadmill here—a place in life where our exertion to be playful feels as though it brings us no closer to our goal—it is only a problem during the initial cultivation of the virtue. After developing playfulness further along, the naturalness with which one acts provides a way off the treadmill. Learning curves exist, even for games. But once the game is learned, the enjoyment deepens. Additionally, the mere existence of a learning curve—and the cognitive drag on initial flights—does nothing to shoot down playfulness.

Moreover, the alternative of being unreflective about leisure, or using non-cognitive standards or faculties, seems worse. It takes judgment to organize the many personal and social demands that we have. Feeling things out or doing the most convenient things will not always lead to the best behavior. A good example of needing cognition and social support is mild depression. I deal with this. And when in a rut, the last things that I want to do are eat healthily, work out, or socialize. But those are exactly the things that dig me out. Often, I can do what I need by thinking through things and motivating myself. Sometimes, though, friends and physicians help me along. What I hope this shows is that emotions cannot be counted on in all circumstances. And it is often our own cognition, as well as the cognition and support of others, that helps us through things more reliably.

Mood and Emotional Aspects

However, playfulness is not all in the thinking parts of the brain. *Mood* and *emotions* matter too. I think Aristotle could affirm some aspects of contemporary behavioral science on this topic. For example, psychologist Mark Davis found that the creativity so crucial to playfulness is at its peak when a player is excited but not too excited. If a player is hyper-excitable, his thinking is disordered. But if he is not excited at all, then creativity lags.[30] Philosophers who have studied playfulness also agree. For example, Lukáš Mareš and Emily Ryall take as essential to playfulness positive mental states such as energy, enthusiasm, spontaneity, and anticipation, and Michael Ridge highlights the centrality of fun.[31] Moritz Schlick also emphasized the importance of mood and emotion in playing when he argued that the meaning of life lay in the joy of playing.[32] Moods and emotions matter because they can undermine playfulness or distract from it entirely.

Additionally, mood can distinguish mean-spirited play from genuine play. Psychologist Nina Lieberman observed that, in children, she could distinguish between friendly teasing and caustic mockery by observing the moods of those involved. Mockery and bullying had ill effects. But friendly teasing was consistent with children who could be spontaneous, joyful, and humorous. Playful children seemed more creative in positive-mood contexts.[33] This work on moods led biologists Patrick Bateson and Paul Martin to distinguish playful play from general play. For Bateson and Martin, playful play involves a positive mood, which inclines animals to spontaneous and flexible behavior. By contrast, in the bad forms of play, the mood is different, and the creative spontaneity withers.[34]

Relaxation and Unselfing

The last psychological component of playfulness that I want to discuss is *relaxation*. Aristotle noticed that one of the limits of pleasure is fatigue of our faculties. We get tired, even when doing things that we love, and there is no way to sustain pleasures continuously (*EN* 1175a5-7). Taken generally, this point argues that we need rest, even in positive contexts and from pleasurable experiences.

During her leisure, the playful person participates in activities that rest and renew her to face life. This can happen in many ways, depending on the context. Sometimes, a playful person will select leisure activities that provide an environment that allows her more control, autonomy, or power than her non-leisurely life, as in a game of *Minecraft* or a hike through a familiar trail. This can rest her from a chaotic career or lifestyle. Oppositely, a playful person might choose leisure activities that provide unpredictability, spontaneity, and novelty. If her career or life is monotonous, improvisational comedy or immersive art installations like Meow Wolf can restore wonder. And in yet different circumstances, a playful person may shun structured activities or packed itineraries in order to provide herself with time to do nothing except spend it however she wants when she arrives at that moment. So-called "time affluence" is crucial to life satisfaction. Just having a spot in your schedule where you can enjoy a coffee or a nap in a hammock can make you feel more in control and afford you a chance to appreciate life.[35]

Philosopher Jules Evans takes these observations further by arguing for the necessity of ecstatic experiences, times when our consciousness expands outside of the self, both leaving the troubles and limits of the self behind and moving beyond to find new possibilities for the self. These experiences, he argues, can heal and inspire us, and they may be found anywhere as diverse as a movie theater or mosh pit.[36] Aristotle noticed the same phenomenon. He ends his *Politics* with a discussion about music, and he condones for some people the use of inspiring, passionate melodies that whip some people into mystic frenzies that appear to purge and heal them from harmful emotions (*Pol.* 1341b32-1342a11).

Iris Murdoch called a similar process "unselfing," which she found essential to living well. She details an example where she is brooding over some damage done to her reputation. Anxious and full of resentment, she stares out of her window. But then she sees a kestrel hovering. That moment changes everything. She moves from her anxious, self-obsessed, aching point of view to the kestrel, outside of herself. She simply takes in its beauty and experiences nothing else. Then, when she returns to her self, she is transformed, and the previous matter has lost its importance. She explains later that goodness is connected to *unselfing*, trying to transcend our usual selfish consciousness toward a virtuous consciousness that can see the world as it really is, not as our anxieties and aspirations might have it be.[37] It is precisely in our breaks from psychological or laborious occupations that we come to one of her central realizations:

> By opening our eyes we do not necessarily see what confronts us. We are anxiety-ridden animals. Our minds are continually active, fabricating an anxious, usually self-preoccupied, often falsifying *veil* which partially conceals the world. Our states of consciousness differ in

quality, our fantasies and reveries are not trivial and unimportant, they are profoundly connected with our energies and our ability to choose and act. And if quality of consciousness matters, then anything which alters consciousness in the direction of unselfishness, objectivity, and realism is to be connected with virtue.[38]

Relaxation, even in something as simple letting our mind wander from natural beauty to creative fantasies, can rest us and make us better. By getting outside of ourselves or getting distance from certain experiences, we can return to those matters with a more grounded perspective and renewed resolve. Sometimes, people underestimate the value of rest because of the simplicity of its descriptions: do nothing, stop thinking, just be. But as anyone who meditates will tell you, doing nothing and clearing your mind can be as difficult as they are important.

The main point is that the demands of playfulness are not demands for constant busyness. A virtuous person knows what she needs for flourishing, including taking it easy, for example, by sipping coffee in the sun or sending memes to friends on the phone. In fact, it is quite probable that contemporary playful people in America might choose to do less. There is some empirical evidence to suggest that, despite more leisure time, certain people and families experience more busyness and report that they have less time to enjoy. This runs precisely counter to the value of playfulness (and happiness). While the playful person does have obligations to flourish and to use leisure time well, this does not mean cramming a schedule full of activities. The holistic value of happiness—taken as an entire life lived well by someone with a fully developed personality—is precisely what should prevent a culture of busyness from taking hold.[39] That is why I stressed using happiness in deliberation in the cognitive components above. But here we are talking about feelings and how vital the sense of rest is. I think it has always been a temptation to do more. As far back as 2nd Century Rome, Marcus Aurelius was warning himself about something similar: "If you seek tranquility, do less ... do less, better ... Because most of what we say and do is not essential. If you can eliminate it, you'll have more time, and more tranquility."[40] Similarly, Friedrich Nietzsche in 1800s Germany noticed:

> All of you who are in love with hectic work and whatever is fast, new, strange—you find it hard to bear yourselves, your diligence is escape and the will to forget yourself. If you believed more in life, you would hurl yourself less into the moment. But you do not have enough content in yourselves for waiting—not even for laziness.[41]

In other words, Nietzsche noticed something duplicitous about people who maintain a constant state of busyness and adventure, often in the guise of finding themselves. Here, it is a mock type of playfulness because it looks like play but forgets happiness and virtue generally. Nietzsche rightly criticizes a lot of these people, fraught with fear of missing out, and running from themselves, avoiding who they are. He emphasizes that part of what keeps them from sitting still is that they lack inner content. In this way, laziness becomes a test for these people to sit with their inner emptiness. While I disagree with the hyperbole of Nietzsche, I think that he gets one crucial thing right: people who cannot rest are indicating deep disquiet. This is why Marcus Aurelius recommends doing less as a path toward tranquility. Rest becomes a time for just being where you are. And sometimes, it is not easy to come to terms with where you are. But virtuously playful people do. And they do not judge themselves harshly, nor do they feel the need to do everything at once. Playful people know when and how to sit still.

The point of these qualifications is that relaxation precludes micromanaging and optimizing every microsecond of one's schedule. The playful person will play chess with her friends; the busy person will buy new chess sets, fiddle with the board, order precisely the right drink, etc. The latter looks like being playful, but it is actually erratic and distracted. Like Aristotle said, relaxation prepares us to return to life refreshed (*Pol.* 1337b37-1338a1). From her leisure, the playful person gets new experiences, controlled outlets, social contact, or solitary rest, and any of these can allow her to relax. Sometimes, this means lounging in bed for an extra hour. Sometimes, it means playing chess or hitting the gym. In any case, relaxation renews people to return to non-leisurely life. The benefits apply to more than reinvigorated work or labor; they also apply to social interactions and mundane life. The virtuously playful person uses her leisure in ways that improve her mood, her thinking, and her self, and this reverberates throughout her life.

Characteristics of Playfulness

Beyond these general psychological descriptions, I think playful people exhibit specific characteristics that define them as virtuously playful. At the heart of being playful is a person who can approach her leisure time and its activities with seriousness, creativity, humility, optimism, and sociality, all while avoiding related vices.

Seriousness

A central characteristic of playfulness is *seriousness*. Despite the light mood or relaxing effects, leisure's impact on the self and others shows that a playful person should be serious. This largely comes from the need to consider how to spend leisure time and how to assess its successes or failures. A playful person not only entertains whims, as most do. She is characterized by finding activities, hobbies, and projects to commit herself to, even in small moments of leisure. Sports, liberal arts, home crafts, games, and relationships can all be ways of spending leisure. And the playful person commits herself to these activities, and she puts time enough into the activity to gain basic competence. She strives for improvement and prefers some results and products over others. If she lifts weights during her leisure, for example, she aims to do so safely and effectively. If she bakes, she treats differently the charred chicken pot pie and the croissant that flakes when you open it. Once competent, she makes into her own the activities done and the products finished. She cares about what she does and how what she does reflects her.

By contrast, a *flaky person*—someone who does not commit himself to something to get good at it or to get to know a community—hastily moves on to new activities and lets each frustration or setback end his engagement with the current one. The flaky person is the "ideas man," the person who schemes but never executes. This could be someone who tries dozens of sports but never commits to one long enough to learn its rules. It could be a person who noodles on guitar and learns a couple of chords but never completes a whole song. Casual play is sometimes fine. Yet, if it is *always* casual, a flaky person does not develop the advantages that come with serious engagement. But this is not to say that commitment above everything is characteristic of the playful person.

Obsessiveness can take root in the severe person. The *severe person* stays committed to activities at the neglect of the holistic achievement of happiness or the development of friendships with others. He can take winning too seriously, focusing only on calculable statistics like win percentage or kill-death ratio in Fortnite. Or he could pursue external goods like money or fame rather than cooperation, socialization, or the good of the leisure activity itself. This can burden everything with gravity, or it can leave an audience with the sense that the severe person misses the entire point of playing or having leisure. The severe person does not enjoy much, and he does not play freely or fluidly.

Being playful involves balancing both the flaky and severe impulses. The *playful person* perseveres through challenges; she makes efforts to develop special knowledge, training, and skills; she engages deeply and seriously with the community that plays in the way that she does; and she integrates the play as a facet of her identity.[42] A playful person learns to play competently and understands the reasons for why she plays. She resists the temptation to make play into life or dismiss it as trivial. Play is necessary for living well, but it is not the only thing necessary for living well. The playful person understands this.

Creativity

The playful person is also creative within boundaries, which she sometimes pushes. Here, vices clarify what I mean by creativity. The *rigid person* deleteriously commits himself to the rules in excruciating detail. The narrow focus on the rules prevents him from exploring, communicating openly with other players, or seeing which rules can be stretched in which ways or which activities can be engaged in. A rigid person drains the vivacity from play by treating organic experiences like mechanical operations.

On the other hand, the *unruly person* is equally vicious. He refuses to learn values or honor boundaries. And while his transgressive personality may strike himself as valiantly creative, it is far from that. He cannot create because all he does is criticize; he cannot play because all he does is satisfy his own whims without coordinating with others. The unruly person is irredeemably antisocial, isolated by his own selfish goals to enjoy the game his own way. He is like Johan Huizinga's "spoilsport." Huizinga observes that society tolerates cheaters because they take games seriously (even if winning nefariously). But society, he argues, is disgusted by spoilsports. Spoilsports refuse to play and thus spoil the fun for everyone. Rather than participate in the collective work of playing and maintaining the play world, the spoilsport bursts the imaginative and ludic bubbles, ruining play for everyone involved.[43]

The playful person finds a way between these two vices. She is *creative* because she takes the time to familiarize herself with the hobbies, games, or activities that she is involved in.[44] She develops the skill or intimacy that creativity requires; she respects the activity enough to understand what she engages in; and she learns to perform competently. But then she moves beyond this. By learning the spirit of the hobby, game, or experience, the creative person learns the melody on which she can improvise. She can generate novel ways of realizing the implicit and explicit goals within practices.[45] She learns her craft and then changes it. But no one can change something that she has not respected, nor can she be novel without learning the history of what came before.

Humility

Playfulness involves failure. This happens in learning the initial rules and practices of games or hobbies, as well as exploring new ideas and skills. This necessitates *humility*. As a playful person tries to create and innovate, failure multiplies. But none of the failures deter the truly playful person. She stays committed and coachable.[46]

If failure stops a playful person from learning, exploring, and innovating, then he is fragile. The *fragile person*, in the sense that I am thinking here, avoids failure because he takes failure as indicative of a character flaw, or he assigns too much worth to the opinion of any audience to his failures. This prevents him from persevering, which prevents him from bettering himself, his performance in relevant activities, or the communities that surround either. This is the person who wants to write but cannot stand rereading his own work because the ideas sit stalely, and the prose reads clumsily, not at all like his grandiose inspiration. The mistake is not the failure; rather, it is neglecting to move forward afterward.

But the playful person is not reckless either. The *reckless person* does not learn from failure, and like the spoilsport or the unruly person, he moves from disaster to disaster. The reckless person has no regard for the way in which he plays or the way he uses his leisure, insofar as it takes the brunt of his pent-up energy and frustrations. A reckless person does not mind failure, but he does not mind it because he does not realize he has failed. A fragile person is someone who underestimates his ability and pessimistically surrenders to failure. A reckless person is someone who overestimates his ability and foolishly assumes success, never minding the debris in his path.[47]

By contrast, a playful person learns from failures and moves forward. Her humility allows her not to take herself too seriously, so she can stomach failure's bitter taste. But she also takes herself seriously enough to stay invested in the projects at hand. This allows a proper self-assessment, and it allows her to get good at the skill.

Optimism

Most of the activities that people pursue during leisure involve some amount of uncertainty (as do self-assessment and self-development). No one knows who will win a game for certain. No one can say whether a craft that one works on will turn out as desired. No one can say whether a performance or activity will live up to expectations. For these reasons, the playful person is also *optimistic* about outcomes. She believes that she can win the game, that her craft will turn out given enough practice, and that the experience of going out or doing something will give her what she wants. Leisure and play are training grounds for optimism and managing expectations. This optimism affects everyday life. Overall, optimistic people are more psychologically resilient and vigorous in life. This matters because complex society relies on people believing that the work and coordination it takes to organize everyone will pay off.[48]

Of course, the playful person will not be *naïve*, oblivious to negative influences or obstacles in the way of quality leisure time. The optimistic person can call out unfair games, where someone may be cheating, humiliating opponents, or missing the point of the activity altogether. She can rally against unjust communities and immoral individuals who may discriminate against people wanting to join the activity or play the game. But the injustices of the world would not dull her edge so much that she refuses to cut through the challenges of everyday life. When playful people lose this sense of optimism, they merely go through the motions of leisure activities. Maybe prodigies could be good without the optimism, but few teammates would enjoy playing with a dispirited person, and no good audience would enjoy watching a broken performer.

Sociality

By now, it should be obvious that my conception of playfulness is irreducibly *social*. This also comes from Aristotle. A virtuous person is always sensitive to other people and the ways she directly contributes to others' happiness. Outside (maybe) the virtues of courage, temperance, and wisdom, the majority of Aristotle's virtues are social, regulating our relationships with one another—generosity, magnanimity, mildness in temper, truthfulness in self-presentation, wittiness, and friendliness (*EN* II.7). And of the ten books of *Nicomachean Ethics*, Aristotle dedicates one to justice and two to friendship. After all, Aristotle argues that no person would choose a life full of wealth, power, or any other good, if it somehow prevented her from having friends (*EN* 1155a6-8). And in conditions of political corruption and disarray, as in tyranny, Aristotle says that no friendships would be possible (*EN* 1161a32-4). Without others, we cannot be happy. And even when we have others, if they are not treated justly, we cannot live well either. This is why Aristotle calls us political animals; humans are inseparable from the groups of people that they live with and the institutions they create (*Pol.* 1253a1 ff). And anyone who is completely separable is either a beast or a god, but definitely not a good human.

The playful person, therefore, is sensitive to social considerations. Philosopher María Lugones makes this point when she writes, "Lack of playfulness is not symptomatic of lack of ease but lack of health. I am not a healthy being in 'worlds' that construct me as unplayful."[49] Lugones understands playfulness as something that flows from the self in the presence of other people and the worlds they create and inhabit. When we are playful, we are playful in relation to other people and the worlds we collectively interact in. She argues that when those worlds are harsh, we are not playful, and so part of ourselves wilts. Lugones therefore characterizes the ideal of playfulness as "loving playfulness." The loving attitude constitutes part of the disposition for her. Lugones argues that we must be loving because the self is at stake. She specifies that being lovingly playful involves being open to many things: surprises, being a fool, self-construction, and re/construction of the worlds that we inhabit. It involves interacting with one another despite uncertainty, sacred rules being challenged, firm aspects of ourselves being open to change, and the selves of others and their worlds being open to change as well.[50] I agree with Lugones that playfulness involves others, and if we do not take them into consideration, we cannot be playful. Ignoring others, or mistreating them, means that we are not playing or being playful.[51] So, even though some leisure activities might be solitary, obtaining leisure and using that time invariably involve social considerations. Playful people are aware of how their play affects themselves and others in both their presence and absence.[52]

I am not necessarily describing just laws and institutions here, but more small-scale senses of justice in personal virtue and social interactions. But playful people undoubtedly help communities become just. What we do in our leisure has wider implications. William James, for example, envisioned a world without war. But unlike pacifists who simply argue that war has no positive effects, he is honest to war's deep ambivalence. It can improve individuals through disciplined, courageous action, and it can unify societies in large-scale cooperative efforts that make people proud. Far from a justification of war, he wants us to find a different activity, practice, or project that gets all the benefits without the horrors.[53] This inspired civil service programs, but it could also espouse better ways of using our leisure. Professional sports leagues, art competitions, and international charity efforts could do the same, as might video games. Games researcher Jane McGonigal defends the idea that serious gamers make deep social connections with people that they play with, and they find ways of being connected to bigger projects that other people also find meaningful.[54] Increasingly, leisure activities are explicitly connected to the most significant aspects of our lives, not only as individuals but also as communities. Increasingly, in our leisure activities, we wake up to the world and begin to refuse to be satisfied with traditional values and social arrangements.

But before we can revolutionize, we must have some sort of vision. Ursula K. Le Guin argued why speculative fiction, something many read during their leisure, is so instrumental to justice:

> Hard times are coming, when we'll be wanting the voices of writers who can see alternatives to how we live now, can see through our fear-stricken society and its obsessive technologies to other ways of being, and even imagine real grounds for hope. We'll need writers who can remember freedom—poets, visionaries, realists of a larger reality. ... We live in capitalism, its power seems inescapable—but then, so did the divine right of kings. Any human power can be resisted and changed by human beings. Resistance and change often begin in art. Very often in our art, the art of words.[55]

For Le Guin, writers of fantasy and science fiction dare to challenge the base assumptions of society and therefore reality. Whenever writers spend time inventing utopias, and whenever readers inhabit their realities, people begin to believe that things could be different. Insidious forms of oppression go unchallenged because the social arrangements that sustain them seem obvious. But when we spend our leisure imagining other worlds, we gain new fulcrums to lift away contemporary burdens to clear space for a better future. Emil Cioran states the point more dramatically, "We must be thankful to the civilizations which have not taken an overdose of seriousness, which have played with values and taken their pleasure in begetting and destroying them."[56] Playful people learn values and use them fluidly, but they also actively pursue alternatives and abandon obsolescence. In the buffet of life and social arrangements, playful people have sampled all the dishes, and they are less likely to fixate on one because it is familiar. Philosopher Michael Ridge says it best, "Playfulness is thus transgressive and generates an exhilarating sense of freedom."[57] Again, I hope that I have not made playfulness seem like it is justice in the macro sense; it is not necessarily so legally or institutionally focused. But given the far-reaching effects of self-improvement and community engagement, no just society will lack playful people.

Playfulness and a Good Life

I have given no strict definitions of "play" or "leisure," nor have I tried to categorize all of the activities that a playful person might do. Instead, I have argued that to face our leisure time well, we need to be playful. And to be playful, we must be serious, creative, humble, optimistic, and social. Playful people use their leisure time to move themselves closer to happiness. My hope is that the practical orientation of playfulness and its relation to character, flourishing, and justice side-step many of the concerns for defining precisely play, rest, idleness, leisure, sport, art, or whatever we do in our free time. The sketch of playfulness offered here connects everything to happiness. And I think this connection to happiness shows why contemporary people need to safeguard leisure and consider its use as diligently as we consider fear, pleasure, friendship, wealth, justice, or any of the perennial concerns of philosophy. It is during our leisure that we find intrinsic enjoyment in activities, and it is during our leisure that we can shape ourselves into better people and form intimate and strong communities.

My theory has implications for people as individuals and as groups. As an individual, the playful person stays committed to leisure activities to learn about them as much as she can, to push them forward, and to socialize with other people. Being playful means that she cares to use her leisure time for enjoyable self-exploration and self-improvement. But a playful person is not solipsistic. Being playful also means being sensitive to the social demands of justice. Despite bullies using the justification of "just playing around," exclusionary or destructive play deserves repudiation. In some ways, I part with everyday uses of the term "playful." Colloquially, "playful" is comfortably allied with mischievous or outright malicious people. But on this Aristotelian account, "playfulness" must be nested within the context of a person's life and her journey toward happiness, and it must also be nested within concerns for the health of our communities. Playfulness makes leisure answerable to the concerns of developing a good character and working toward justice.

I can imagine that critics will wonder whether what I have described as playfulness is a misnomer. Whenever we call someone "playful," they might ask, do we really mean that she is fundamentally and foremost someone who uses her leisure well? However, I know of no other word to use. And I know of no other framework than a virtue of playfulness to organize the panoply of claims about play and its corresponding arena of leisure. In this broad area of life that we all face, it seems that playfulness can serve as a guide for assessing our behavior. And without a guide, I think that we risk getting lost on the way to happiness.

So, what can my guide do? First, I think it offers a way to organize the divided opinions of philosophers on play. Why might Heraclitus or Rousseau champion play? They understand the deeply creative, cooperative, and optimistic ways that play impacts life. These things encourage us to develop ourselves, to help others, and to savor many of life's experiences. Philosophers who champion play rightly emphasize the positive aspects. Why, then, do Plato and Aristotle criticize some forms of play so harshly? They understand that play, with the wrong mood and motivations, can train people to be recalcitrant to new ideas, mean-spirited toward others, and indulgent in their own impulses. They rightly notice that play is not amoral, and its moral stakes can be used for exploitation and exclusion just as much as enjoyment, self-improvement, or authenticity. Both camps of philosophers are sensitive to the moral stakes of play. And playfulness, as a character trait, helps us to assess the multivalent ethical aspects of our characters in relation to leisure and living well. Leisure can renew us, shelter us in life's storms, and provide a showcase for life's joys. But leisure also presents opportunities for us to become callous, unjust, and attuned to the wrong things in life. The ambivalence of play, and any of the activities taken up in leisure, shows exactly why playfulness is useful here. Assessing the activity of play in relation to the character trait of playfulness contextualizes the intrinsically enjoyable activities within the moral pursuit of living well with others. Focusing on playfulness, rather than play, gives us a vantage to assess play. Seriousness, creativity, humility, optimism, and sociality are dimensions for measuring leisure activities in the space of morality.

Second, my book not only deals with philosophy and scholarly opinion. I think that it deals with history and the future, figuring out how to assess real examples of human behavior. My book is a proposal that we keep two questions in mind when evaluating the ethical and political implications of leisure activities: (1) Can someone who does that thing remain a properly playful person? And (2) can someone live a full, flourishing human life while doing that activity? Making moral assessments of play would need to hold up to the scrutiny of both.

Let us consider some examples to see how this works. First, consider history. Romans slew prisoners in creative games in the Colosseum; Catholic officials tortured heretics with innovative engineering; Nazi physicians invented novel experiments for castration and torture in extreme conditions. But should we call these perpetrators playful, even if they did these things with glee? On my theory, no. They fail various aspects of the character trait defined here. These behaviors developed in the perpetrators many vicious thoughts, feelings, and motivations. Their actions took them further away from flourishing. And on the criteria of playfulness, they fail especially the social requirement. So, while these vicious examples of play may be creative in some ways, they would never be playful on my account. Playfulness is firmly fixed to a person's own wellbeing, and because a person's wellbeing is attached to the wellbeing of her community, the trait must be assessed holistically and historically. And I would say that the decline of Rome, the conquests of Catholic countries, and World War II Germany all show precisely why such 'playful' people did not flourish. It is only when actions of play or instances of creativity are abstracted away from particular persons and their historical circumstances that they can be judged as 'playful.' The particularity must be heeded. The impacts of the playful activities must be connected to how they affect the players and the people around them. When this is done, these counterexamples fail the criteria I laid out. But these are relatively clear cases of unplayful behavior.

I also think that my theory can offer new ways of assessing novel and difficult cases. For example, consider Marco Evaristti's art piece "Helena." Evaristti arranged ten brand new blenders in a row, all plugged in, all immaculate, all sporting a yellow button that would clearly turn the blenders on. Inside each blender's pitcher were two things: water and a live, swimming goldfish. Anyone viewing the exhibit could see what would happen if they activated the switch, and they had every opportunity to do so. Authorities shut the installation down after two days. But sixteen goldfish died in the meantime. In my mind, there is no doubt that Evaristti was using his leisure to make art and play. I would even say that he was properly serious. He learned his craft. He was properly creative. No one had done this before. He was even humble and optimistic enough to get the installation approved and displayed in a museum in Denmark. But also in my mind, there is no doubt that he was not playful, at least in my sense of the term. He failed to take many things into consideration. First, I do not think that he appreciated what his art said about him as a person. (Maybe he did not care. But that does not bode well either.) Second, I do not think that he appreciated how his play would affect the goldfish, the people in the museum who flipped the switches, or the people in the audience of the spectacle. All of this shows disregard for what I have called "sociality," and it shows why art and play are rightly nested within ethical categories. My criteria for playfulness offer a way of beginning a conversation about why this case is unsettling.[58]

But my theory also has something to say about more ambiguous cases, such as enjoying art that portrays villains as attractive, or spending ample time with the kind of art that Plato would have expelled from the *kallipolis* or that Aristotle might have beat people for. Should playful people enjoy Vladamir Nabokov's erotic descriptions of a prepubescent girl or Cormac McCarthy's account of Judge Holden's murders and rapes? The issues here are complicated and long-standing, and I can offer no definitive solution.[59] However, even though this account will not settle the debates about the moral evaluation of art or games, it can offer new metrics by which to assess them. On the terms laid out here, the immoral effects must be demonstrable. It must be shown how certain activities affect our habits and how that detracts, if it does, from our achievement of happiness. Aristotelians always play an empirical game in ethics and politics. And in weighing the im/morality of play, the empirical evidence must do the heavy lifting, and the life-long goal of happiness must do the judging. There are no in-principle judgments here, only probabilities for defilement of character or demolition of happiness. We must in good faith ask: Does this person who enjoys these activities in this way end up worse off as a direct result of the activity? It must be specific. A person who reads McCarthy for allusions to Dante or Melville differs from a person who reads McCarthy because the violence is cool and he would like to be Judge Holden. Same for *American Psycho* or *Wolf of Wall Street* or *The Joker*, or any artwork where toxic people clearly miss the point.

My examples so far have been negative. But supposedly good things deserve scrutiny too, such as Aristotle's most celebrated leisure activity: contemplating theory, especially as done by philosophers. Even if my theory properly denounces immoral uses of leisure, would I say that philosophy should be evaluated in terms of playfulness? Is philosophy just another leisure activity? First, for nonprofessional philosophers, yes, philosophy is done during leisure, so I do think that playfulness evaluates it. And insofar as the philosophy is serious, creative, humble, optimistic, and social, I would call it properly playful. I think the best forms of philosophy are. Good philosophy must be all those things to climb the icy heights of reason and apply the knowledge from the celestial realm to the teeming, balmy world of prudence. But is this a relegation of philosophy to mere leisure activity? I do not think so. Calling the best forms of philosophy playful is only an insult for those who do not understand how important being playful is. In judging philosophy by playfulness, I emphasize the question of whether philosophy might rightly be integrated into a life lived well. Playfulness will likely cut against some forms of academic, professionalized philosophy at universities today. And instead it would advocate for the philosophy that the ancient world knew: concerns about the deep nature of daily life, puzzles about how we investigate ideas, and assessments of the values that we hold for whether they help us to live well. Ancient philosophy was public, social, and consistently applied to everyday life. This is not to insult contemporary philosophy and its specialized tasks any more than it is to insult contemporary microbiology for its esoteric investigations of cellular mechanisms and organic chemical reactions. It is just to say that philosophy, in the broad way that the ancients understood it, is very much a part of a playful person's life, or really anyone who explicitly evaluates her own life. Ask an athlete or a musician what makes for the best and worst people in her field, and you will get a philosophy of her specialization. Philosophy, in the narrow sense that academics and administrators refer to in colleges, is not necessary for living well. When Aristotle celebrated philosophy and theory, I do not think that he had in mind what gets published in most top-tier journals today. I think that Aristotle had in mind the literal meaning of the words that he used. *Philosophia* comes from *philia*, meaning love, and *sophia*, meaning wisdom. *Theōria* comes from *theōreō*, the verb for spectating or contemplating, a verb just as appropriate describing the audience of a play, an ambassador at a political event, or a philosopher thinking. The point is not abstruseness. The point is participating in, reflecting on, and making sense of everything. When deeming intellectual activity necessary for a good life, I think Aristotle meant philosophy and theory in these broader senses.[60] *Philosophia* and *theōria* are the activities of neither brutes nor snobs. They are the activities of people who can immerse themselves in a singular moment and then reflect on what that moment means; they are the activities of people who play and let that play affect their thinking about life.

During the COVID pandemic, we saw very clearly that those who could not sit with themselves and their thoughts and explore fictional worlds fared much worse than those who could. Thought, including imagination, touches every aspect of life. But Aristotle knew we were so much more than thinking things. We have bodies that must grow and reproduce. We have desires that push and pull us. We have emotions that attract and repulse us toward and away from life's cornucopia of goods. We have motivations and dispositions that bias our thoughts and give momentum to our actions. And we are not people, in the full sense of the term, apart from friends, fellow citizens, and the complex interactions we have with people all over the world. Aristotle, no doubt, was an intellectualist, holding that reason is the supreme faculty that organizes everything. But leaders have nothing without followers, and followers can always push back. Humans are complex, and Aristotle knew this. To read him only as an intellectual with academic concerns is to abandon his complex psychology and ambivalent assessments of most things in life. And to see philosophy as only what credentialed philosophers do is to forget the original meanings of the terms involved.

Leisure affects our lives. Without it, no person is happy. But if a person only spends his leisure watching *The Office* while browsing Facebook and Instagram on his cell phone, he has missed the point of life. We may do this on occasion. But if we never delve more seriously into crafts, activities, or games that challenge us and bring us closer to other people, we waste opportunities to understand ourselves and others, as well as to improve our own lives and the lives of others. Playfulness as a virtue deserves as much consideration as the classical virtues like courage, temperance, and justice. And play, as an activity, deserves investigation as much as other activities like making money and friends. If we neglect playfulness and what it teaches us about our characters and the goals of our lives, we neglect reflection on a crucial aspect of being human. Aristotle said that humans are political. Marx said that humans are productive. I say that humans are playful. Happy people are playful people. And no happy person fails at playing well.

Notes

1 Patrick Bateson and Paul Martin, *Play, Playfulness, Creativity, and Innovation* (Cambridge: Cambridge University Press, 2013), esp. pp. 19–20, 72–4. Sergio Pellis and Vivien Pellis, *The Playful Brain: Venturing to the Limits of Neuroscience* (Oxford: Oneworld, 2009), esp. pp. 68–78. Another noteworthy case: some male orangutans use play and grooming to initiate mating. Dominant, large male orangutans can emit "long calls," loud calls that reverberate throughout forests. Females move toward them from vast distances. Smaller males know that they cannot compete with larger ones. So, they instead find females, follow them, and interact with them playfully. After a while, the female may choose to allow the male to mate with her. Medium-sized males, by contrast, might intercept a female on the way to a dominant male and rape her. P. 152. This behavior might support the idea that dominant animals do not need to be as playful, clever, or imaginative and instead can rely on coercion or brute desirability. This finding likely applies to humans to some degree. A recent study by Justin Brienza and Igor Grossman suggests that higher-class humans reason less wisely than lower-class ones. "Social Class and Wise Reasoning about Interpersonal Conflicts across Regions, Persons, and Situations." *Proceedings of the Royal Society B*, vol. 284, iss. 1869 (Dec 2017): pp. 1–9.
2 See: Alison Gopnik, *The Philosophical Baby: What Children's Minds Tell Us About Truth, Love, and the Meaning of Life* (New York: Farrar, Straus, and Giroux, 2009), esp. pp. 27–31, 221–9, 244.

3 Shalom H. Schwartz, "Are There Universal Aspects in the Structure and Contents of Human Values?" *Journal of Social Issues*, vol. 50, no. 4 (1994): pp. 19–45; Frank W. Wicker, Frank B. Lambert, Frank C. Richardson, and Joseph Kahler, "Categorical Goal Hierarchies and Classification of Human Motives," *Journal of Personality*, vol. 52, iss. 3 (Sept 1984): pp. 285–305. For a complication of what "leisure" means in other cultures, see: Garry Chick, "Leisure and Culture: Issues for an Anthropology of Leisure," *Leisure Studies*, vol. 20 (1988): pp. 111–33. See also: Aristotle, *EN* 1176b32-3, 1177a2-10; *Pol.* 1337b37-1338a1.
4 Stuart Brown, "How Does Play Shape Our Development?" interview by Guy Raz, *TED Radio Hour*, 27 March 2015, https://www.npr.org/transcripts/395065944.
5 For two recent treatments of the value of play, see: Avery Kolers, "The Grasshopper's Error: Or, on How Life Is a Game," *Dialogue*, vol. 54 (2016): pp. 727–46; Michael Ridge, "Why So Serious? The Nature and Value of Play," *Philosophy and Phenomenological Research*, vol. 105 (2022): pp. 406–34.
6 See: Martha Nussbaum, "Non-Relative Virtues: an Aristotelian Approach," in *Moral Disagreements: Classic and Contemporary Readings*, ed. Christopher W. Gowans (London: Routledge, 2000), p. 168–71.
7 I substitute "manliness" for "courage" here because I think it shows the negative and gendered aspects of *andreia* more clearly, perhaps a message that Aristotle meant to communicate.
8 For a contemporary defense of the importance of leisure, see: Julie L. Rose, *Free Time* (Princeton: Princeton University Press, 2016).
9 See: Jenny Odell, *How to Do Nothing: Resisting the Attention Economy* (Brooklyn: Melville House, 2019).
10 See: Brian O'Connor, *Idleness: A Philosophical Essay* (Princeton: Princeton University Press, 2018). See also: J. S. Russell, "Idleness as Play and Leisure: A Reflection on *Idleness: A Philosophical Essay* by Brian O'Connor," *American Journal of Play*, vol. 14, no. 3 (2022): pp. 304–26.
11 See: Bernard Suits, "Words on Play," *Journal of the Philosophy of Sport*, Appendix I: Presidential Address, vol. 4, iss. 1 (1977): pp. 117–31; Ridge, "Why So Serious?"
12 Annette Holba calls these activities "leisure." I have opted for their characterization rather than the label to avoid equivocation and confusion. "In Defense of Leisure," *Communication Quarterly*, vol. 62, no. 2 (2014): pp. 179–92.
13 For general debates about leisure, see: Tony Blackshaw, ed., *Routledge Handbook of Leisure Studies* (London: Routledge, 2015); Chris Rojek, Susan B. Shaw, and A. J. Veal, eds., *A Handbook of Leisure Studies* (New York: Palgrave Macmillan, 2006); Josef Pieper, *Leisure: The Basis of Culture* (San Francisco: Ignatius: 2009). For philosophical debates about leisure, see: Alexander Sager, "The Philosophy of Leisure" in: *The Routledge International Handbook of Leisure Studies*, ed. Tony Blackshaw (London: Routledge, 2013); Johan Bouwer and Marco van Leeuwen, *Philosophy of Leisure: Foundations of the Good Life* (London: Routledge, 2017); Tom Winnifrith and Cyril Barrett, ed., *The Philosophy of Leisure* (New York: Palgrave Macmillan, 1989). For problematization of definitions of leisure, see: Tony Blackshaw, *Leisure* (London: Routledge, 2010); Karl Spracklen, *Constructing Leisure: Historical and Philosophical Debates* (New York, Palgrave Macmillan, 2011).
14 Blackshaw, *Leisure*, p. 120; Bouwer and van Leeuwen, *Philosophy of Leisure*, p. 230.
15 Sarah Broadie, "Taking Stock of Leisure" in: *Aristotle and Beyond: Essays on Metaphysics and Ethics* (Cambridge: Cambridge University Press, 2007), p. 198.
16 On the curiosity of industrialized and post-industrialized civilizations not needing to work as hard as they do, see: Clive Jenkins and Barrie Sherman,

The Collapse of Work (London: Methuen, 1979). For a discussion of contemporary societies killing leisure by filling it with superficiality, see: Jonathan Gershuny, "Are We Running out of Time?" *Futures*, vol. 24, no. 1 (Jan./Feb. 1992), pp. 3–22; Lonnie Golden, "Comment on Jonathan Gershuny, 'Are we running out of time?'" and Jonathan Gershuny, "Reply from J. I. Gershuny" *Futures*, vol. 24, no. 1 (Jan./Feb. 1992): pp. 203–7.

17 Michael Argyle, *The Psychology of Happiness*, 2nd ed., (London: Routledge, 2001): pp. 223–4. Christopher Peterson, *A Primer in Positive Psychology* (Oxford: Oxford University Press, 2006), pp. 92–4. Qinglong Shao, "Does Less Working Time Improve Life Satisfaction? Evidence from European Social Survey," *Health Economics Review*, vol. 12, iss. 50 (Sept. 2022).

18 This loose definition of leisure follows closely: Sager, "The Philosophy of Leisure," pp. 5–14. But Max Kaplan offers seven criteria essential to leisure. Leisure serves the opposite function of work's economic functions. Its possessors expect leisure to be pleasant and remember it fondly. Leisure has minimal involuntary social obligations. It is intimately tied to a psychological perception of freedom. The activities of leisure can range from frivolous to serious. And lastly, leisure often includes an element of play. *Leisure in America: A Social Inquiry* (New York: Wiley, 1960): pp. 22–5. The quick discussion of leisure activities comes from Amy Wrzesniewski, Paul Rozin, and Gwen Bennett's discussion of "passions." "Working, Playing, and Eating: Making the Most of Most Moments," in: *Flourishing: Positive Psychology and the Life Well-Lived*, ed. Corey L.M. Keyes and Jonathan Haidt (Washington, DC: American Psychological Association, 2003): pp. 188–93. Their discussion of passions also shows why it is difficult to think of work as being the opposite of leisure. Work, when a mere job or career, will never trump leisure time. But when work is a calling, and when that work engages a person's passions, it can be a source of incredible fulfillment. This is why my definition above relies more on necessity and survival than on labor or exchange.

19 See: Bernard Lefkowitz, *Breaktime: Living without Work in a Nine-to-Five World* (New York: Penguin, 1979).

20 For example, hedonists can argue that leisure should maximize pleasure, economists can argue that leisure should maximize individual preferences, and perfectionists can argue that leisure should develop the self excellently. See: Sager, "Philosophy of Leisure," pp. 9–11.

21 Evidence suggests that TV and computer use can have detrimental effects on children's lives, while physical activity tends to improve childhood health. For example, TV can affect children's sleep patterns, and social media can deteriorate mental health in adolescents. Contrastingly, physical activity seems to reduce depression and anxiety while improving cognitive function and self-esteem. See: E. Juulia Paavonen, Marjo Pennonen, Mira Roine, Satu Valkonen, and Anja Riita Lahikainen, "TV Exposure Associated with Sleep Disturbances in 5- to 6-Year-Old Children," *Journal of Sleep Research*, vol. 15, iss. 2 (2006): pp. 154–61; Gwenn Schurgin O'Keeffe, Kathleen Clarke-Pearson, and the Council on Communications and Media, "Clinical Report—The Impact of Social Media on Children, Adolescents, and Families," *The American Academy of Pediatrics*, vol. 127, no. 4 (Apr 2011): pp. 800–4; Stuart J. H. Biddle and Mavis Asare, "Physical Activity and Mental Health in Children and Adolescents: A Review of Reviews," *British Journal of Sports Medicine*, vol. 45, iss. 11 (2011): pp. 886–895.

22 Argyle, *Happiness*, ch. 8. Relatedly, some scholars argue that vulgar art might pacify a subjugated class, acting as diversion and escape, which keeps them from understanding how ideology or propaganda blinds them to political problems. See: Theodor Adorno and Max Horkheimer, "The Culture Industry: Enlightenment

and Mass Deception" in: *Dialectic of Enlightenment: Philosophical Fragments* (Stanford: Stanford University Press, 2002), pp. 94–115.
23 For example, skydiving has a risk of one fatality for every 130,000 jumps. But if a novice decides to skydive in tandem with an instructor—literally fastened to the instructor who deploys the parachute for both of them—the risk falls to one in 500,000 jumps. United States Parachute Association, "Skydiving Safety" https://uspa.org/Find/FAQs/Safety; A. Westman, M. Rosén, P. Berggren, U. Björnstig, "Parachuting from Fixed Objects: Descriptive Study of 106 Fatal Events in BASE Jumping 1981–2006," *British Journal of Sports Medicine*, vol. 42, no. 6 (Jun. 2008): pp. 431–6.
24 See: Ollie Gillman, "'Alcoholic' Iranian Could Be Granted Refugee Status in Australia over Fears He Will Be Executed for Drinking Booze If He Goes Home," *Daily Mail* (26 Dec 2016): http://www.dailymail.co.uk/news/article-4067154/Alcoholic-Iranian-granted-refugee-status-executed-drinking-booze-home.html; Hugh Tomlinson, "Ashtiani Freed after 9 Years on Death Row," *The Times* (19 March 2014): https://www.thetimes.co.uk/article/ashtiani-freed-after-9-years-on-death-row-5gk8c3nnds7.
25 Plato, *Republic*, X. Aristotle, *Pol.*, 1336a29-b12.
26 George Santayana, *Three Philosophical Poets: Lucretius, Dante, and Goethe*, Critical Edition, The Works of George Santayana, Vol. VIII (Cambridge, MA: The MIT Press, 2019), p. 127.
27 C. Thi. Nguyen, *Games: Agency as Art* (Oxford: Oxford University Press, 2020), p. 199; chs. 9–10.
28 Psychologist Michael J. Apter distinguishes between "telic" and "paratelic" activities. Telic activities have explicit goals and are purposive, such as serious study, charity, political and religious activities, collecting, finishing DIY projects, or taking classes. Paratelic activities are ones where the actor seeks excitement foremost, such as movies, games, parties, going to bars and clubs, listening to music, socializing with friends, fishing, or taking a vacation. As paraphrased by: Argyle, *Psychology*, p. 129.
29 For a short description of the hedonic treadmill, see: Seneca, "On the Happy Life," trans. John Davie (Oxford: Oxford University Press, 2008), sec. 1. Alison Gopnik describes a ludic equivalent when writing, "The fundamental paradox of play is that in order to be able to reach a variety of new goals in the long run, you have to actively turn away from goal seeking in the short run." "In Defense of Play," *The Atlantic* (12 Aug. 2016): https://www.theatlantic.com/education/archive/2016/08/in-defense-of-play/495545/.
30 Mark A. Davis, "Understanding the Relationship between Mood and Creativity: A Meta-analysis," *Organizational Behavior and Human Decision Processes*, vol. 108, iss. 1 (Jan. 2009): esp. pp. 28–9.
31 Lukáš Mareš and Emily Ryall, "'Playing Sport Playfully': on the Playful Attitude in Sport," *Journal of the Philosophy of Sport*, vol. 48, no. 2 (2021): p. 296. They also include curiosity, creativity, and a desire to experience fun and enjoyment. Michael Ridge, "Fun and (Striving) Games: Playfulness and Agential Fluidity," *Journal of the Philosophy of Sport*, vol. 48, no. 3 (2021): p. 408. He also notes that playfulness requires a sense of safety and lack of anxiety. pp. 411–2.
32 Moritz Schlick, "On the Meaning of Life," trans. Peter Heath, in: *Philosophical Papers*, vol. II [1925–1936], ed. H. Mulder and Barbara F. B. van de Velde-Schlick (Dordrecht, Holland: D. Reidel Publishing Company, 1979), p. 114.
33 J. Nina Lieberman, *Playfulness: Its Relationship to Imagination and Creativity* (New York: Academic Press, 1977).
34 Bateson and Martin, *Play*, p. 13.

35 For a discussion of how time affluence impacts well-being, see: Tim Kasser and Kennon M. Sheldon, "Time Affluence as a Path toward Personal Happiness and Ethical Business Practice: Empirical Evidence from Four Studies," *Journal of Business Ethics*, vol. 84, suppl. 2, Working to Live or Living to Work (2009): pp. 243–55.
36 Jules Evans, *The Art of Losing Control: A Philosopher's Search for Ecstatic Experience* (Edinburgh: Canongate, 2017), esp. Introduction.
37 Iris Murdoch, *The Sovereignty of Good* (London: Routledge, 2002), pp. 82–91.
38 Murdoch, *Sovereignty*, p. 82.
39 See: Anthony P. Graesch, "Material Indicators of Family Busyness," *Social Indicators Research*, vol. 93, no. 1, Time Use and Qualities of Life (Aug. 2009): pp. 85–94.
40 Marcus Aurelius, *Meditations*, trans. Greogry Hays (New York: Modern Library, 2004), IV.24.
41 Friedrich Nietzsche, *Thus Spake Zarathustra: A Book for All and None*, trans. Adrian Del Caro (Cambridge: Cambridge University Press, 2006): p. 32.
42 Here, I am following closely what Robert A. Stebbins calls "serious leisure:" "Serious Leisure: A Conceptual Statement," *The Pacific Sociological Review*, vol. 25, no. 2 (Apr. 1982): pp. 256–7.
43 Johan Huizinga, *Homo Ludens: A Study of the Play-Element in Culture* (Kettering, OH: Angelico Press, 2006): p. 11.
44 For an overview of some of the main claims of the research on creativity, see: Stephen J. Dubner, "Where Does Creativity Come from (and Why Do Schools Kill It off)? [Ep. 355]" *Freakonomics Radio* (24 Oct. 2018): http://freakonomics.com/podcast/creativity-2/.
45 For a discussion of human creativity in scientific literature, see: Bateson and Martin, *Play*, ch. 5. There they discuss the work of J. P. Guilford, who distinguishes between converging and diverging styles of thought. Convergent thinkers are critical and analytical, bringing ideas together for comparison. But the divergent thinker is open to and generates new ideas. They also discuss Paul Torrance who described creativity as having three parts: fluency (the number of different ideas that a person can generate), flexibility (the ability of a person to use different ways of thinking to address ideas in many domains), and originality (the measure of novelty of the ideas generated and the ability of a person to generate new ideas without relying on routine or habit). It is also important to note that sometimes creative people can be taken as spoilsports. But creative players usually do not break the rules as much as find ambiguities or vagueness that they can use to push play forward. This leads to innovation in games and arts. A great example is Pop Warner and Carlisle Academy's Native American students' influence on football. See: Sally Jenkins, *The Real All Americans* (New York: Doubleday, 2007); David M. Nelson, *The Anatomy of a Game: Football, the Rules, and the Men who Made the Game* (Newark: University of Delaware Press, 1994), esp. p. 127; Jad Abumrad and Robert Krulwich, hosts, "American Football," *RadioLab*, WNYC Studios (28 January 2015): https://www.wnycstudios.org/story/football/.
46 In behavioral sciences, sometimes researchers use the 50/50 rule for a fair game. A fair game between two animals is one where each animal is equally likely to win. But in gaming literature, this might also relate to difficulty and flow. Mihaly Csikszentmihalyi studied extensively the relationship between the difficulty of an activity and the degree of enjoyment. If a person is engaging in an activity that is too easy for him, then he will be bored and not enjoy himself. Similarly, if a person is doing something that is too difficult for him, he will be anxious and also not enjoy himself. It is precisely when the

activity is just beyond one's present ability that it is most pleasurable. These activities exercise one's skills, motivate one to improve, and allow one to cope with the challenges in that activity. The other major contributor to an activity's pleasure is the social component. The more social the activity, the more people generally enjoy it. See: Argyle, *The Psychology of Happiness*, p. 128; Bateson and Martin, *Play*, p. 61.

47 This is not a neat analogy to playfulness, but it is similar enough to mention. The difference between a fragile and reckless person might be analogized to the opposite ends of the Dunning-Kruger Effect. People at the beginning of learning a skill tend to overestimate their own ability because they have no idea how wrong they are or how complicated the skill gets. People who are experts tend to underestimate their expertise and assume others have similar knowledge. They know how wrong they could be and assume others do too. Or, as Bertrand Russell once wrote, "The fundamental cause of the trouble is that in the modern world the stupid are cocksure while the intelligent are full of doubt." "The Triumph of Stupidity" in: *Mortals and Others* (London: Routledge, 2009), p. 204.

48 Peterson, *A Primer*, ch. 5, esp. pp. 129–30.

49 María Lugones, "Playfulness, 'World-Travelling,' and Loving Perception," *Hypatia*, vol. 2, no. 2 (1987): p. 14.

50 Lugones, "Playfulness," pp. 16–7.

51 Some critics might think that I am assuming a strong unity of the virtues that to have one virtue fully, one may need all virtues fully. For example, they might say that my account of playfulness assumes that playful people also have the virtues of justice and friendliness, even though they are separate virtues. This concern seems right, but I do not know how strong I want to make the claim here.

52 Reflecting on his love of crossword puzzles, Jeffrey Tlumak raised two points to me. First, he asked whether sociality could be imagined. I am non-committal with respect to this. Literature and some games rely on imagined characters or players. So, it seems like imagined communities would be good in similar ways to real-life interactions. But with sociality, I am most concerned with people neglecting others who could be included or helped through play. That leads to Tlumak's second question, which is whether there can be phases in life, such that at one point someone is social enough to justify more solitary practices later in life. Here, this seems plausible to me within a certain limit. People need others. And sociality here need not involve taxing interactions. But it also seems that solitary activity is permissible. The most important aspect of the social requirement of playfulness is that it keeps people from being malevolent, neglectful, or otherwise socially detached. The solitary person is not necessarily any of these. He might just choose to disengage, and that would be permissible, on the same grounds as rest. But it is when a person is solitary, as well as misanthropic, miserly, and unconcerned with others, that the social aspect is transgressed.

53 William James, "The Moral Equivalent of War" in: *Pragmatism and Other Essays* (New York: Washington Square, 1968).

54 Jane McGonigal, *Reality is Broken: Why Games Make Us Better and How They Can Change the World* (New York: Penguin, 2011), esp. chs. 5–6.

55 Le Guin argued this in her 2014 acceptance speech of the National Book Foundation's Medal for Distinguished Contribution to American Letters. "Full Speech: Ursula K. Le Guin's Passionate Defense of Art over Profits," *American Masters PBS* (26 July 2019): youtube.com.

56 Emil Cioran, "Civilization and Frivolity," in: *A Short History of Decay*, trans. Richard Howard (New York: Arcade, 2012): p. 8.

57 Ridge, "Fun," p. 412.
58 For a pedagogical discussion of Evaristti's piece, see: Tomaz Zupancic, "Contemporary Artworks and Art Education," *International Journal of Education through Art*, vol. 1, no. 1 (2005): pp. 34–5.
59 See: Berys Gaut, *Art, Emotion, and Ethics* (Oxford: Oxford University Press, 2007); Richard A. Posner, "Against Ethical Criticism," *Philosophy and Literature*, vol. 21, no. 1 (Apr. 1997): pp. 1–27; Michael Kammen, *Visual Shock: A History of Art Controversies in American Culture* (New York: Vintage Books, 2006).
60 For discussion on intellect's centrality in Aristotelian ethics, see: Anne Jeffrey, *Being and Becoming Good: On the Diversity of Human Goodness and Virtue* (Oxford: Oxford University Press, forthcoming); Martha Nussbaum, "Aristotle on Human Nature and the Foundations of Ethics" in: *World, Mind, and Ethics: Essays on the Ethical Philosophy of Bernard Williams*, eds. J. E. J. Altham and Ross Harrison (Cambridge: Cambridge University Press, 1995), ch. 6.

Conclusion
Happy People Play, Playful People Live

Playfulness is the virtuous ability to regulate our leisure time. Playful people approach their leisure with a sense of seriousness, creativity, humility, optimism, and sociality. They play, rest, develop themselves, and engage their communities, all in service of living better lives and cultivating more justice. Playful people therefore stand a better chance at attaining happiness, and happy people are always playful. The stakes are high with playfulness. Playfulness is about free time—not only in the sense of being free from necessity but also in the sense of practicing our freedom.

I hope that my theory explains why Aristotle thought play a *pharmakon*, both a medicine and a drug. It is all about the dose. Playful people

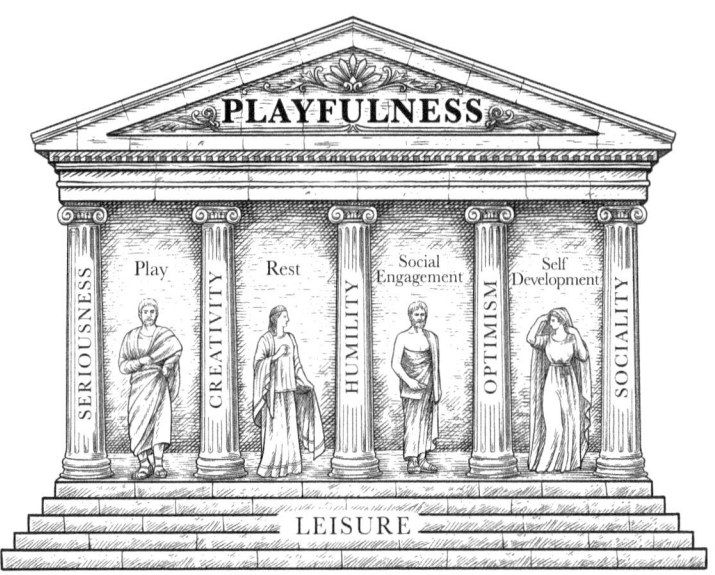

Figure 5.1 "The Temple of Playfulness" by Kelelowor. An illustration of the virtue of playfulness.

play much differently than nonplayful people. Nonplayful people are worth scrutinizing because they squander leisure. Playful people are worth celebrating because they use leisure to improve their characters and cultivate justice. They get life, and their leisure shows this. Playful activities teach us to be human. In rest, we sit with our mortality and cherish human finitude. In play, limits fall away, and we transcend ourselves. In engaging others, we rehearse social roles and experiment with new ways of being human. If we are lucky, a significant portion of our time is dedicated to leisure, and in that arena, we do well to equip the virtue of playfulness. In the game of life, the end is death. Playfulness ensures that we do some living in the meantime.[1]

Note

1 On the game of life, see: Avery Kolers, "The Grasshopper's Error: Or, on How Life Is a Game," *Dialogue*, vol. 54 (2016): pp. 727–46.

References

Abumrad, Jad and Robert Krulwich, hosts. "American Football." *RadioLab*, WNYC Studios. 28 January 2015. https://www.wnycstudios.org/story/football/

Adorno, Theodor and Max Horkheimer. "The Culture Industry: Enlightenment and Mass Deception." In: *Dialectic of Enlightenment: Philosophical Fragments*, eds. Gunzelin Schmid Noerr, Trans. Edmund Jephcott. Stanford: Stanford University Press, 2002, pp. 94–115.

Alfano, Mark. *Character as Moral Fiction*. Cambridge: Cambridge University Press, 2013.

Annas, Julia. *The Morality of Happiness*. Oxford: Oxford University Press, 1993.

———. "Virtue Ethics." In: *The Oxford Handbook of Ethical Theory*, ed. David Copp. Oxford: Oxford University Press, 2006. Ch. 18.

Ariely, Dan, George Loewenstein, and Drazen Prelec. "Tom Sawyer and the Construction of Value." *Journal of Economic Behavior & Organization*, vol. 60 (2006): pp. 1–10.

Argyle, Michael. *The Psychology of Happiness*, 2nd ed. London: Routledge, 2001.

Aristophanes. *Clouds*. Trans. W. J. M. Starkie. London: MacMillan and Co., 1911.

———. *Lysistrata*. Adapted and arranged by Winifred Ayres Hope. New York: Samuel French, 1915.

Aristotle. *Aristotle in 23 Volumes*. Trans. Horace Rackham. Vol. 21. Cambridge, MA: Harvard University Press, n.d.-a Uploaded to Perseus Digital Library, 1934. http://perseus.tufts.edu/

———. *The Complete Works of Aristotle: The Revised Oxford Translation*, ed. Jonathan Barnes. Princeton: Princeton University Press, 1984.

———. *Categories*. Trans. J. L. Ackrill. In: *The Complete Works of Aristotle: The Revised Oxford Translation*, ed. Jonathan Barnes. Princeton: Princeton University Press, 1984.

———. *Eudemian Ethics*. Trans. J. Solomon. In: *The Complete Works of Aristotle: The Revised Oxford Translation*, ed. Jonathan Barnes. Princeton: Princeton University Press, 1984.

———. *Magna Moralia*. Trans. St. G. Stock. In: *The Complete Works of Aristotle: The Revised Oxford Translation*, ed. Jonathan Barnes. Princeton: Princeton University Press, 1984.

———. *Metaphysics*. Trans. W. D. Ross. In: *The Complete Works of Aristotle: The Revised Oxford Translation*, ed. Jonathan Barnes. Princeton: Princeton University Press, 1984.

References

———. *Nicomachean Ethics*. Trans. W. D. Ross. Rev. by J. O. Urmson. In: *The Complete Works of Aristotle: The Revised Oxford Translation*, ed. Jonathan Barnes. Princeton: Princeton University Press, 1984.
———. *On the Soul*. Trans. W. D. Ross. In: *The Complete Works of Aristotle: The Revised Oxford Translation*, ed. Jonathan Barnes. Princeton: Princeton University Press, 1984.
———. *Politics*. Trans. B. Jowett. In: *The Complete Works*, ed. Barnes.
———. *Rhetoric*. Trans. W. Rhys Roberts. In: *The Complete Works*, ed. Barnes.
Aurelius, Marcus. *Meditations*. Trans. Gregory Hays. New York: Modern Library, 2003.
Badhwar, Neera K. "The Limited Unity of Virtue." *Noûs*, vol. 30, no. 3 (Sept. 1996): pp. 306–29.
Bakhtin, Mikhail. *Rabelais and His World*. Trans. Helene Iswolsky. Bloomington: Indiana University Press, 1984.
Barbalet, J. M. "Boredom and Social Meaning." *British Journal of Sociology*, vol. 50, no. 4 (Dec. 1999): pp. 631–46.
Barthes, Roland. *S/Z: An Essay*. Trans. Richard Miller. New York: Hill and Wang, 1974.
Bateson, Patrick and Paul Martin. *Play, Playfulness, Creativity, and Innovation*. Cambridge: Cambridge University Press, 2013.
Bench, Shane W. and Heather C. Lench. "On the Function of Boredom." *Behavioral Sciences*, vol. 3 (2013): pp. 459–72.
Beiser, Frederick C. *German Idealism: The Struggle against Subjectivism*. Cambridge, MA: Harvard University Press, 2002.
Bekoff, Marc. "Social Play Behavior: Cooperation, Fairness, Trust, and the Evolution of Morality." *Journal of Consciousness Studies*, vol. 8, no. 2 (2001): pp. 81–90.
Berlyne, D. E. *Conflict, Arousal, and Curiosity*. McGraw-Hill Series in Psychology. New York: McGraw-Hill, 1960.
Biddle, Stuart J. H. and Mavis Asare. "Physical Activity and Mental Health in Children and Adolescents: A Review of Reviews." *British Journal of Sports Medicine*, vol. 45, no. 11 (2011): pp. 886–895.
Blackshaw, Tony. *Leisure*. London: Routledge, 2010.
Blackshaw, Tony, ed. *Routledge Handbook of Leisure Studies*. London: Routledge, 2015.
Bourdieu, Pierre. *Distinction: A Social Critique of the Judgment of Taste*. Trans. Richard Nice. London: Routledge, 2010.
Bouwer, Johan and Marco van Leeuwen. *Philosophy of Leisure: Foundations of the Good Life*. London: Routledge, 2017.
Brienza, Justin P. and Igor Grossman. "Social Class and Wise Reasoning about Interpersonal Conflicts across Regions, Persons, and Situations." *Proceedings of the Royal Society B*, vol. 284, no. 1869 (Dec. 2017): pp. 1–9.
Broadie, Sarah. "Taking Stock of Leisure." In: *Aristotle and Beyond: Essays on Metaphysics and Ethics*. Cambridge: Cambridge University Press, 2007, ch. 12.
Brown, Stuart. "How Does Play Shape Our Development?" Interview by Guy Raz, *TED Radio Hour*, 27 March 2015. https://www.npr.org/transcripts/395065944
———. "Play Is More Than Fun." Filmed May 2008 at the Art Center Design Conference. *TED Video*, 26:42, Published online 2009. https://youtu.be/HHwXlcHcTHc

References

Brudney, Daniel. "Community and Completion." In: *Reclaiming the History of Ethics: Essays for John Rawls*, ed. Andrews Reath, Barbara Herman, and Christine M. Korsgaard. Cambridge: Cambridge UP, 1997, pp. 388–415.

Bruni, Tommaso, Matteo Mameli, and Regina A. Rini. "The Science of Morality and Its Normative Implications." *Neuroethics*, vol. 7 (2014): pp. 159–72.

Burghardt, Gordon. *The Genesis of Animal Play: Testing the Limits*. Cambridge, MA: The MIT Press, 2006.

Cashen, Matthew. "The Ugly, the Lonely, and the Lowly: Aristotle on Happiness and the External Goods." *History of Philosophy Quarterly*, vol. 29, no. 1 (Jan. 2012): pp. 1–19.

Chick, Garry. "Leisure and Culture: us for an Anthropology of Leisure." *Leisure Studies*, vol. 20 (1988): pp. 111–33.

Cioran, Emil. "Civilization and Frivolity." In: *A Short History of Decay*, trans. Richard Howard. New York: Arcade, 2012a.

———. *The Temptation to Exist*. Trans. Richard Howard. New York: Arcade, 2012b

Curd, Patricia, ed. *A Presocratics Reader: Selected Fragments and Testimonia*, 2nd ed. Trans. Richard D. McKirahan and Patricia Curd. Indianapolis: Hackett, 2011.

Davis, Mark A. "Understanding the Relationship between Mood and Creativity: A Meta-analysis." *Organizational Behavior and Human Decision Processes*, vol. 108, no. 1 (Jan. 2009): pp. 25–38.

Derrida, Jacques. *Dissemination*. Trans. Barbara Johnson. Chicago: University of Chicago Press, 1981.

Destrée, Pierre. "Education, Leisure, and Politics." In: *The Cambridge Companion to Aristotle's Politics*, ed. Marguerite Deslauriers and Pierre Destrée. Cambridge: Cambridge University Press, 2013, ch. 12.

Doris, John. *Lack of Character: Personality and Moral Behavior*. Cambridge: Cambridge University Press, 2002.

Dreier, Peter. "The Real Story of Baseball's Integration that You Will not See in *42*." *The Atlantic*. 11 Apr. 2013. https://www.theatlantic.com/entertainment/archive/2013/04/the-real-story-of-baseballs-integration-that-you-wont-see-in-i-42-i/274886/

Dubner, Stephen J. "Where Does Creativity Come from (and Why Do Schools Kill It off)? [Ep. 355]." *Freakonomics Radio*. 24 Oct. 2018. http://freakonomics.com/podcast/creativity-2/

Eberle, Scott G. "The Elements of Play: Toward a Philosophy and a Definition of Play." *Journal of Play*, vol. 6, no. 2 (2014): pp. 214–33.

Edwards, Jonathan. "A Transplant Surgeon Used an Electric Beam to Burn His Initials into Patients' Organs. He Just Lost His Medical License." *The Washington Post*. 31 Jan. 2022. washingtonpost.com

Elpidorou, Andreas. "The Bored Mind is a Guiding Mind: Toward a Regulatory Theory of Boredom." *Phenomenology and the Cognitive Sciences*, vol. 17, no. 3 (2018): pp. 455–84.

Epictetus. *The Handbook*. Trans. Nicholas P. White. Indianapolis: Hackett, 1983.

Euripides. *Grief Lessons: Four Plays*. Trans. Anne Carson. New York: New York Review Book, 2006.

Evans, Jules. *The Art of Losing Control: A Philosopher's Search for Ecstatic Experience*. Edinburgh: Canongate, 2017.

Feezell, Randolph. "A Pluralistic Conception of Play." In: *The Philosophy of Play*, eds. Ryall, Emily, Wendy Russell, and Malcolm MacLean. London: Routledge, 2014. Ch. 1.
Fisher, Cynthia D. "Boredom at Work: What, Why, and What Then?" In: *The Social Functions of Emotion and Talking about Emotion at Work*, ed. Dirk Lindebaum, Deanna Geddes, and Peter J. Jordan. Cheltenham: Edward Elgar Publishing, 2018. Ch. 4.
Flaubert, Gustave. *Madame Bovary*, Second Norton Critical Edition. New York: W. W. Norton, 2005.
Foot, Philippa. *Natural Goodness*. Oxford: Clarendon Press, 2001.
———. *Virtues and Vices*. Oxford: Oxford University Press, 2002.
Fosty, George and Darril Fosty. *Black Ice: The Lost History of the Colored Hockey League of the Maritimes, 1895–1925*. New York: Stryker-Indigo, 2004.
"Full Speech: Ursula K. Le Guin's Passionate Defense of Art over Profits." *American Masters PBS*. 26 July 2019. youtube.com
Gabriel, Shira, Esha Naidu, et al. "Creating the Sacred from the Profane: Collective Effervescence and Everyday Activities." *The Journal of Positive Psychology*, vol. 15, no. 1 (2020): pp. 129–54.
Gadamer, Hans-Georg. *Truth and Method*, 2nd Rev. Ed. Trans. Joel Weinsheimer and Donald G. Marshall. London: Continuum.
Gaut, Berys. *Art, Emotion, and Ethics*. Oxford: Oxford University Press, 2007.
Geertz, Clifford. "Deep Play: Notes on the Balinese Cockfight." *Daedalus*, vol. 101, no. 1 (1972): pp. 1–37.
Gershuny, Jonathan. "Are We Running out of Time?" *Futures*, vol. 24, no. 1 (Jan/Feb. 1992): pp. 3–22.
Gillman, Ollie. "'Alcoholic' Iranian Could Be Granted Refugee Status in Australia over Fears He Will Be Executed for drinking Booze If He Goes Home." *Daily Mail*. 26 Dec 2016. http://www.dailymail.co.uk/news/article-4067154/Alcoholic-Iranian-granted-refugee-status-executed-drinking-booze-home.html
von Goethe, Johann Wolfgang. *Götz von Berlichingen*. 1773. Uploaded to *Spiegel Online*. http://gutenberg.spiegel.de/buch/geschichte-gottfriedens-von-berlichingen-mit-der-eisernen-hand-3621/4
Golden, Lonnie and Jonathan Gershuny. "Comment on Jonathan Gershuny, 'Are We Running Out of Time?' and 'Reply from J. I. Gershuny'." *Futures*, vol. 24, no. 1 (Jan./Feb. 1992): pp. 203–7.
Gopnik, Alison. "In Defense of Play." *The Atlantic*. 12 Aug. 2016. https://www.theatlantic.com/education/archive/2016/08/in-defense-of-play/495545/
———. *The Philosophical Baby: What Children's Minds Tell Us About Truth, Love, and the Meaning of Life*. New York: Farrar, Straus, and Giroux, 2009.
Gottlieb, Paula. "Aristotle's 'Nameless' Virtues." *Apeiron*, vol. 27, no. 1 (1994): pp. 1–16.
Graesch, Anthony P. "Material Indicators of Family Busyness." *Social Indicators Research*, vol. 93, no. 1, Time Use and Qualities of Life (Aug. 2009): pp. 85–94.
Gray, Peter. *Free to Learn: Why Unleashing the Instinct to Play Will Make Our Children Happier, More Self-Reliant, and Better Students of Life*. New York: Basic Books, 2013.
Gregory, Alice. "Running Free in Germany's Outdoor Preschools." *The New York Times Style Magazine*. 18 May 2017. https://www.nytimes.com/2017/05/18/t-magazine/germany-forest-kindergarten-outdoor-preschool-waldkitas.html

Gruendel, Aileen D. and William J. Arnold. "Influence of Preadolescent Experiential Factors on the Development of Sexual Behavior in Albino Rats." *Journal of Comparative and Physiological Psychology*, vol. 86, no. 1 (1974): pp. 172–8.

Hamlyn, D. W. "Aristotle on Dialectic." *Philosophy*, vol. 65, no. 254 (Oct. 1990): pp. 465–76.

Heinaman, Robert, ed. *Aristotle and Moral Realism*. Boulder: Westview Press, 1995.

Hesiod. *Works and Days*. In: *Theogony* and *Works and Days*, trans. M. L. West. Oxford: Oxford World Classics, 2008.

Hirji, Sukaina. "What's Aristotelian about Neo-Aristotelian Virtue Ethics?" *Philosophy and Phenomenological Research*, vol. 98, no. 3 (May 2019): pp. 671–98.

Horwitz, Steven. *Hayek's Modern Family*. New York: Palgrave Macmillan, 2015.

Huffman, Aaron, Evan Sult, Jeff Lin, and Sean Nelson. "Flagpole Sitta." *Where Have All the Merrymakers Gone?* Los Angeles: Slash, 1997.

Huizinga, Johan. *Homo Ludens: A Study of the Play-Element in Culture*. Kettering, OH: Angelic Press, 2016.

Hume, David. *Enquiry Concerning the Principles of Morals*, ed. Tom L. Beauchamp. Oxford: Clarendon, 2010.

———. *Treatise of Human Nature*, ed. David Fate Norton and Mary J. Norton. Oxford: Clarendon, 2011.

Hunnicutt, Benjamin K. "The History of Western Leisure." In: *A Handbook of Leisure Studies*, ed. Chris Rojek, Susan M. Shaw, and A.J. Veal. New York: Palgrave Macmillan, 2006, ch. 4.

Hurka, Thomas. *Perfectionism*. New York: Oxford University Press, 1993.

Hurka, Thomas and John Tasioulas. "Games and the Good." *Proceedings of the Aristotelian Society*, vol. 80 (2006): pp. 217–64.

Hursthouse, Rosalind. *On Virtue Ethics*. Oxford: Oxford University Press, 1999.

———. "The Virtuous Agent's Reasons: A Reply to Bernard Williams." In: *Aristotle and Moral Realism*, ed. Heinaman, Robert. Boulder: Westview Press, 1995. pp. 24–33.

James, William. "The Moral Equivalent of War." In: *Pragmatism and Other Essays*. New York: Washington Square, 1968.

Jeffrey, Anne. *Being and Becoming Good: On the Diversity of Human Goodness and Virtue*. Oxford: Oxford University Press, forthcoming.

Jenkins, Clive and Barrie Sherman. *The Collapse of Work*. London: Methuen, 1979.

Jenkins, Sally. *The Real All Americans*. New York: Broadway Books, 2007.

Johnson, Steven. *Wonderland: How Play Made the Modern World*. New York: Riverhead Books, 2016.

Kammen, Michael. *Visual Shock: A History of Art Controversies in American Culture*. New York: Vintage Books, 2006.

Kant, Immanuel. *Metaphysics of Morals*. Trans. Mary J. Gregor. In: *Practical Philosophy*, ed. Mary J. Gregor, intro. Allan Wood. Cambridge: Cambridge UP, 1996.

———. "On a Supposed Right to Lie Because of Philanthropic Concerns." In: *Ethical Philosophy*, 2nd ed., trans. James W. Ellington. Indianapolis: Hackett, 1994, pp. 162–6.

Kaplan, Max. *Leisure in America: A Social Inquiry*. New York: Wiley, 1960.

Kasser, Tim and Kennon M. Sheldon. "Time Affluence as a Path toward Personal Happiness and Ethical Business Practice: Empirical Evidence from Four Studies." *Journal of Business Ethics*, vol. 84, suppl. 2, Working to Live or Living to Work (2009): pp. 243–55.

Kolers, Avery. "The Grasshopper's Error: Or, on How Life Is a Game." *Dialogue*, vol. 54 (2016): pp. 727–46.

Kyle, Donald G. *Sport and Spectacle in the Ancient World*, 2nd ed. West Sussex: Wiley Blackwell, 2015.

Laertius, Diogenes. *Lives of Eminent Philosophers*. Trans. Pamela Mensch. Oxford: Oxford University Press, 2018.

Lefkowitz, Bernard. *Breaktime: Living without Work in a Nine-to-Five World*. New York: Penguin, 1979.

Liddell, Henry George, Robert Scott, and Henry Stuart Jones. *A Greek-English Lexicon*. Uploaded to *Perseus Digital Library*, ed. Gregory R. Crane. http://www.perseus.tufts.edu/hopper/

Lieberman, J. Nina. *Playfulness: Its Relationship to Imagination and Creativity*. New York: Academic Press, 1977.

Lipscomb, Benjamin J. B. *The Women Are Up to Something: How Elizabeth Anscombe, Philippa Foot, Mary Midgley, and Iris Murdoch Revolutionized Ethics*. Oxford: Oxford UP, 2022.

Louden, Robert. "On Some Vices of Virtue Ethics." *American Philosophical Quarterly*, vol. 21, no. 3 (July 1984): pp. 227–36.

Lugones, María. "Playfulness, 'World'-Travelling, and Loving Perception." *Hypatia*, vol. 2, no. 2 (Summer 1987): pp. 3–19.

MacCumhaill, Clare and Rachael Wiseman. *Metaphysical Animals: How Four Women Brought Philosophy Back to Life*. New York: Doubleday, 2022.

Machiavelli, Niccolò. *Discourses on the First Decade of Titus Livius*. Trans. Ninian Hill Thomson. London: Kegan Paul, Trench, and Co., 1883.

MacIntyre, Alasdair. *After Virtue*, 3rd ed. South Bend, IN: University of Notre Dame Press, 2008.

———. *Dependent Rational Animals: Why Human Beings Need the Virtues*. Chicago: Open Court, 1999.

Mareš, Lukáš and Emily Ryall. "'Playing Sport Playfully': on the Playful Attitude in Sport." *Journal of the Philosophy of Sport*, vol. 48, no. 2 (2021): pp. 293–306.

Martin, Marion, Gaynor Sadlo, and Graham Stew. "The Phenomenon of Boredom." *Qualitative Research in Psychology*, vol. 3 (2006): pp. 193–211.

Marx, Karl. *German Ideology*. Amherst: Prometheus Books, 1998.

McDonald, Soraya Nadia. "Audio of Bill Cosby Joking about Drugging Women Resurfaces." *The Washington Post*. 18 Nov. 2014. https://www.washingtonpost.com/news/morning-mix/wp/2014/11/18/audio-of-bill-cosby-joking-about-drugging-women-resurfaces/

Meisner, Dwayne A. *Orphic Tradition and the Birth of the Gods*. Oxford: Oxford University Press, 2018.

Miller, Christian. *Character and Moral Psychology*. Oxford: Oxford University Press, 2014.

Morwood, James and John Taylor, ed. *The Pocket Oxford Classical Greek Dictionary*. Oxford: Oxford University Press, 2002.

Mozart, Wolfgang Amadeus. "Leck mic him Arsch." Canon, B-flat major. 1792.

Mulfinger, Nadine, Sabine Müller, et al. "Honest, Open, Proud for Adolescents with Mental Illness: Pilot Randomized Controlled Trial." *Journal of Child Psychology and Psychiatry*, vol. 59, no. 6 (05 Dec. 2017): pp. 684–91.

Murdoch, Iris. *The Sovereignty of Good*. London: Routledge, 2002.

Neate, Rupert. "Goldman Sachs Restricts Intern Workday to 17 Hours in Wake of Burnout Death." *The Guardian*. 17 Jun. 2015. https://www.theguardian.com/business/2015/jun/17/goldman-sachs-interns-work-hours

Nehamas, Alexander. "Plato and the Mass Media." *The Monist*, vol. 71, no. 2 (Apr. 1988): pp. 214–34.

Neijzen, Mara. "The Accessibility of Moral Virtue in the Context of Depressive Episodes." *The Journal of Ethics*, vol. 27 (2023): pp. 393–414.

Nietzsche, Friedrich. *Thus Spake Zarathustra: A Book for All and None*, trans. Adrian Del Caro. Cambridge: Cambridge University Press, 2006.

Nelson, David M. *The Anatomy of a Game: Football, the Rules, and the Men who Made the Game*. Newark: University of Delaware Press, 1994.

Nguyen, C. Thi. *Games: Agency as Art*. Oxford: Oxford University Press, 2020.

———. "Philosophy of Games." *Philosophy Compass*, vol. 12, no. 8 (Aug. 2017): pp. 1–18.

Nietzsche, Friedrich. *Beyond Good and Evil*. Trans. Walter Kaufmann. New York: Vintage, 1989.

———. *The Gay Science*. Trans. Josefine Nauckhoff. Cambridge: Cambridge University Press, 2001.

Notopoulos, James A. "The Name of Plato." *Classical Philology*, vol. 34, no. 2 (Apr. 1939): pp. 135–45.

Nussbaum, Martha C. "Aristotelian Social Democracy." In: *Liberalism and the Good*, ed. R. Bruce Douglass, Gerald M. Mara, and Henry S. Richardson. New York: Routledge, 1990, ch. 10.

———. "Aristotle on Human Nature and the Foundations of Ethics." In: *World, Mind, and Ethics: Essays on the Ethical Philosophy of Bernard Williams*, ed. J. E. J. Altham and Ross Harrison. Cambridge: Cambridge University Press, 1995. Ch. 6.

———. *The Fragility of Goodness: Luck and Ethics in Greek Tragedy and Philosophy*, Updated ed. Cambridge: Cambridge University Press, 2001.

———. "Nature, Function, and Capability: Aristotle on Political Distribution." *Oxford Studies in Ancient Philosophy*, suppl. vol. I (1988): pp. 145–84.

———. "Non-Relative Virtues: an Aristotelian Approach." In: *Moral Disagreements: Classic and Contemporary Readings*, ed. Christopher W. Gowans. London: Routledge, 2000a, pp. 168–71.

———. *Women and Human Development: The Capabilities Approach*. Cambridge: Cambridge University Press, 2000b, pp. 78–80.

O'Brien, Wendell. "Boredom." *Analysis*, vol. 47, no. 2 (Apr. 2014): pp. 236–44.

O'Connor, Brian. *Idleness: A Philosophical Essay*. Princeton: Princeton University Press, 2018.

Odell, Jenny. *How to Do Nothing: Resisting the Attention Economy*. Brooklyn: Melville House, 2019.

O'Keeffe, Gwenn Schurgin, Kathleen Clarke-Pearson, and the Council on Communications and Media. "Clinical Report—The Impact of Social Media on Children, Adolescents, and Families." *The American Academy of Pediatrics*, vol. 127, no. 4 (Apr. 2011): pp. 800–4.

Oldenberg, Ray. *The Great Good Place: Cafés, Coffee Shops, Bookstores, Bars, Hair Salons, and Other Hangouts at the Heart of a Community*. Boston: Marlowe & Company, 1999.

Otto, Beatrice K. *Fools Are Everywhere: The Court Jester around the World*. Chicago: The University of Chicago Press, 2007.

Paavonen, E. Juulia, Marjo Pennonen, Mira Roine, Satu Valkonen, and Anja Riita Lahikainen. "TV Exposure Associated with Sleep Disturbances in 5- to 6-Year-Old Children." *Journal of Sleep Research*, vol. 15, no. 2 (2006): pp. 154–61.

Pieper, Josef. *Leisure: The Basis of Culture*. San Francisco: Ignatius: 2009.

Pellis, Sergio and Vivien Pellis. *The Playful Brain: Venturing to the Limits of Neuroscience*. Oxford: Oneworld, 2009.

Peterson, Christopher. *A Primer in Positive Psychology*. Oxford: Oxford University Press, 2006.

Plato. *Plato: Complete Works*, ed. John M. Cooper. Indianapolis: Hackett, 1997.

———. Laws. Trans. Trevor J. Saunders. In: *Complete Works*, ed. Cooper.

———. Republic. Trans. G. M. A. Grube. Rev. C. D. C. Reeve. In: *Complete Works*, ed. Cooper.

Posner, Richard A. "Against Ethical Criticism." *Philosophy and Literature*, vol. 21, no. 1 (Apr. 1997): pp. 1–27.

Reginster, Bernard. "Nietzsche is New Happiness: Longing, Boredom, and the Elusiveness of Fulfillment." *Philosophic Exchange*, vol. 37, no. 1, art. 2 (2006–7): pp. 17–25.

Ridge, Michael. "Fun and (Striving) Games: Playfulness and Agential Fluidity." *Journal of the Philosophy of Sport*, vol. 48, no. 3 (2021): pp. 403–13.

———. "Why So Serious? The Nature and Value of Play." *Philosophy and Phenomenological Research*, vol. 105 (2022): pp. 406–34.

Rojek, Chris, Susan M. Shaw, and A. J. Veal, ed. *A Handbook of Leisure Studies*. New York: Palgrave Macmillan, 2006.

Rose, Julie L. *Free Time*. Princeton: Princeton University Press, 2016.

Rousseau, Jean-Jacques. *Emile: Or on Education*. Trans. Allan Bloom. New York: Basic Books, 1979.

Royal Society for Public Health. *#StatusOfMind: Social Media and Young People's Mental Health and Wellbeing*. 19 May 2017. https://www.rsph.org.uk/about-us/news/instagram-ranked-worst-for-young-people-s-mental-health.html

Russell, Bertrand. *The Conquest of Happiness*. New York: Liveright, 2013.

———. "The Triumph of Stupidity." In: *Mortals and Others*. London: Routledge, 2009.

Russell, J.S. "Idleness as Play and Leisure: A Reflection on *Idleness: A Philosophical Essay* by Brian O'Connor." *American Journal of Play*, vol. 14, no. 3 (2022): pp. 304–26.

Ryall, Emily. "Playing with Words: Further Comment on Suits' Definition." In: *The Philosophy of Play*, eds. Ryall, Emily, Wendy Russell, and Malcolm MacLean. London: Routledge, 2014. Ch. 3.

Ryall, Emily, Wendy Russell, and Malcolm MacLean, ed. *The Philosophy of Play*. London: Routledge, 2014.

Ryzik, Melena, Cara Buckley, and Jodi Kantor. "Louis C.K. Is Accused by 5 Women of Sexual Misconduct." *The New York Times*. 9 Nov. 2017. https://www.nytimes.com/2017/11/09/arts/television/louis-ck-sexual-misconduct.html

Sager, Alexander. "The Philosophy of Leisure." In: *The Routledge International Handbook of Leisure Studies*, ed. Tony Blackshaw. London: Routledge, 2013, ch. 1.
Santayana, George. *Three Philosophical Poets: Lucretius, Dante, and Goethe*, Critical ed. The Works of George Santayana, Vol. VIII. Cambridge, MA: The MIT Press, 2019.
Saujani, Reshma. *Brave, Not Perfect: Fear Less, Fail More, and Live Bolder*. New York: Penguin, 2019.
Schlick, Moritz. "On the Meaning of Life." Trans. Peter Heath. In: *Philosophical Papers*, vol. II [1925–1936], ed. H. Mulder and Barbara F. B. van de Velde-Schlick. Dordrecht, Holland: D. Reidel Publishing Company, 1979. pp. 112–29.
Schopenhauer, Arthur. *The World as Will and Representation*. Trans. E. F. J. Payne. Vol. I. New York: Dover 1969.
Schwartz, Shalom H. "Are There Universal Aspects in the Structure and Contents of Human Values?" *Journal of Social Issues*, vol. 50, no. 4 (1994): pp. 19–45.
Seneca. *On the Happy Life*. Trans. John Davie. Oxford: Oxford University Press, 2008.
Shao, Qinglong. "Does Less Working Time Improve Life Satisfaction? Evidence from European Social Survey." *Health Economics Review*, vol. 12, no. 50 (Sept. 2022).
Shenk, David. "What Is the Flynn Effect, and How Does It Change Our understanding of IQ?" *WIREs Cognitive Science*, vol. 8 (Jan.-Apr. 2019): p. e1366.
Sicart, Miguel. *Play Matters*. Cambridge, MA: The MIT Press, 2014.
Singer, Peter. "Famine, Affluence, and Morality." *Philosophy and Public Affairs*, vol. 1, no. 3 (Spring 1972): pp. 229–43.
———. *The Most Good You Can Do*. New Haven: Yale University Press, 2015.
Sinnott-Armstrong, Walter, ed. *Moral Psychology: Volume 3: The Neuroscience of Morality: Emotion, Brain Disorders and Development*. Cambridge, MA: The MIT Press, 2008.
Smith, Richard P. "Boredom: A Review." *Human Factors*, vol. 23, no. 3 (1981): pp. 329–40.
Solmsen, Friedrich. "Leisure and Play in Aristotle's Ideal State." *Rheinisches Museum für Philologie*, vol. 107, no. 3 (1964): pp. 193–22.
Spracklen, Karl. *Constructing Leisure: Historical and Philosophical Debates*. New York: Palgrave Macmillan, 2011.
Star Trek: First Contact. Film. Directed by Jonathan Frakes. Los Angeles: Paramount Pictures, 1996.
Stebbins, Robert A. "Serious Leisure: A Conceptual Statement." *The Pacific Sociological Review*, vol. 25, no. 2 (Apr. 1982): pp. 256–7.
Sterba, James P. *The Triumph of Practice Over Theory in Ethics*. Oxford: Oxford University Press, 2004.
Suits, Bernard. *The Grasshopper: Games, Life, and Utopia*. Peterborough: Broadview Press, 2014.
———. "Is Life a Game We Are Playing?" *Ethics*, vol. 77, no. 3 (Apr. 1967): pp. 209–13.
———. "Words On Play." *Journal of the Philosophy of Sport*, Appendix I: Presidential Address, vol. 4, no. 1 (1977): pp. 117–31.
Svensson, Frans. "Eudaimonist Virtue Ethics and Right Action: A Reassessment." *The Journal of Ethics*, vol. 14, no. 4 (Dec. 2011): pp. 321–39.

References

Swanton, Christine. *Target Centered Virtue Ethics*. Oxford: Oxford University Press, 2021.

———. *Virtue Ethics: A Pluralistic View*. Oxford: Oxford University Press, 2003.

Taylor, T. L. *Watch Me Play: Twitch and the Rise of Game Live Streaming*. Princeton: Princeton University Press, 2018.

Tessman, Lisa. *Burdened Virtues: Virtue Ethics for Liberatory Struggles*. Oxford: Oxford University Press, 2005.

van Tilburg, Wijnan A. P. and Eric R. Igou. "Boredom Begs to Differ: Differentiation from Other Negative Emotions." *Emotion*, vol. 17, no. 2 (2017): pp. 309–22.

Tomlinson, Hugh. "Ashtiani Freed after 9 Years on Death Row." *The Times*. 19 March 2014. https://www.thetimes.co.uk/article/ashtiani-freed-after-9-years-on-death-row-5gk8c3nnds7

Tversky, Amos and Daniel Kahneman. "Judgment under Uncertainty: Heuristics and Biases." *Science*, New Series, vol. 185, no. 4157 (27 Sept. 1974): pp. 1124–31.

Tweedy, Jo. "Inside the Scandinavian-style Forest Schools Where Parents Pay for Children to Learn How to Get Dirty, Play with Knives, and Light Fires." *Daily Mail*. 10 Nov. 2015. http://www.dailymail.co.uk/femail/article-3302171/Inside-Scandinavian-style-forest-schools-parents-PAY-children-learn-dirty-play-knives-light-fires.html

Twenge, Jean M., Thomas E. Joiner, Megan L. Rogers, and Gabrielle N. Martin. "Increases in Depressive Symptoms, Suicide-Related Outcomes, and Suicide Rates Among U.S. Adolescents After 2010 and Links to Increased New Media Screen Time." *Association for Psychological Science: Clinical Psychological Science*, vol. 6, no. 1 (2018): pp. 3–17.

United States Parachute Association. "Skydiving Safety." https://uspa.org/Find/FAQs/Safety

"Vase Number 301645." *Musée du Louvre*. n.d. image hosted on beazley.ox.ac.uk.

Wall, John. "All the World's a Stage: Childhood and the Play of Being." In: *The Philosophy of Play*, eds. Ryall, Emily, Wendy Russell, and Malcolm MacLean. London: Routledge, 2014. Ch. 2.

Wallace, David Foster. "This is Water." Speech delivered at Kenyon College to the Class of 2005, Gambier, Ohio, 21 May, Published online 2013. https://youtu.be/8CrOL-ydFMI

Westman, A., M. Rosén, P. Berggren, and U. Björnstig. "Parachuting from Fixed Objects: Descriptive Study of 106 Fatal Events in BASE Jumping 1981–2006." *British Journal of Sports Medicine*, vol. 42, no. 6 (Jun. 2008): pp. 431–6.

Whitehead, Alfred North. *Process and Reality*, ed. David Ray Griffin and Donald W. Sherburne, Corrected ed. New York: The Free Press, 1978.

Wicker, Frank W., Frank B. Lambert, Frank C. Richardson, and Joseph Kahler. "Categorical Goal Hierarchies and Classification of Human Motives." *Journal of Personality*, vol. 52, no. 3 (Sept 1984): pp. 285–305.

Willett, Cynthia. *Interspecies Ethics*. New York: Columbia University Press.

Williams, Bernard. "Acting as the Virtuous Person Acts." In: *Aristotle and Moral Realism*. ed. Heinaman, Robert. Boulder: Westview Press, 1995. pp. 13–23.

———. *Ethics and the Limits of Philosophy*. Cambridge, MA: Harvard University Press, 1985.

———. "The Makropulos Case: Reflections on the Tedium of Immortality." In: *Problems of the Self: Philosophical Papers 1956–1972*. Cambridge: Cambridge University Press, n.d.-b, Ch. 6.

Winnicott, Donald. *Playing and Reality*. London: Routledge, 2005.
Winnifrith, Tom and Cyril Barrett, ed. *The Philosophy of Leisure*. New York: Palgrave Macmillan, 1989.
Wolf, Susan. "Moral Saints." *The Journal of Philosophy*, vol. 79, no. 8 (Aug. 1982): pp. 419–39.
Wrzesniewski, Amy, Paul Rozin, and Gwen Bennett. "Working, Playing, and Eating: Making the Most of Most Moments." In: *Flourishing: Positive Psychology and the Life Well-Lived*, ed. Corey L.M. Keyes and Jonathan Haidt. Washington, DC: American Psychological Association, 2003, ch. 8.
van Zyl, Liezl. "Virtue Ethics and Right Action." In: *The Cambridge Companion to Virtue Ethics*, ed. Daniel C. Russell. Cambridge: Cambridge University Press, 2013. Ch. 8.
"You Can Discover More About a Person in an Hour of Play than in a Year of Conversation: Plato? Richard Lingard? Anonymous?" Quote Investigator. 30 July 2015. https://quoteinvestigator.com/2015/07/30/hour-play/
Zupancic, Tomaz. "Contemporary Artworks and Art Education." *International Journal of Education through Art*, vol. 1, no. 1 (2005): pp. 29–41.

Index

Pages followed by "n" refer to notes.

aretē see Aristotle virtue
Alala xi
Aristotle: ambivalence about play 23–5; censorship of some art and play 18–9, 22; courage 2–3, 5, 14, 31–2, 37, 56; defense of play for children 13; education 13–4; function argument 35–6; happiness 32–6, 65, 71; importance of experience 32; leisure 14–7, 66–7; luck in happiness 33–4; method in ethics 2–3, 31–2; nameless virtues 31–2; opinion on play 4, 10–1; play as connected to pleasure 19–20; play as insufficient for happiness 22–3; play as medicine 12–7; play as part of happiness 17; play as poison 18–23; temperance 21–2, 27n23, 40; theory and importance of pleasure 20–1; virtue as mean 2–3; virtue's definition 4–6, 36–41, 65; wit 12–3, 21, 26n11

Blink-182 51
bullying and negative play 82
busyness, warning against 74–5

cafes and coffee 6, 72–3
carnivals and jesters 50–1
collective effervescence 51
courage, gender, and failure 55
creativity 90n45

Dionysus 1, 18
doomscrolling 67

ecstatic experiences 73
eudaimonia see happiness

"Enter Sandman" 20
ethical, sense of 5, 29
excellence *see* Aristotle virtue

fart 1, 18
Ferrell, Will 21
flourishing *see* happiness

Greek: art 10; culture 1; play 7; shifting toward leisure 16

happiness 4, 32–6
Heraclitus 9
homies x, 72

idleness 6
imagination 80–1
immoral and unjust play 82–4
it *see* tag

Le Guin, Ursula 7, 80–1
leisure 6–7, 65–70; Aristotle's views 11, 14–7; as connected to playfulness 65–70; as crucial for freedom for Aristotle 15; definition 66, 88n18; empirical work on 67; as necessary for flourishing for Aristotle 16
"Lick Me in the Ass" 51
ludic treadmill 71

Meow Wolf 73
method 2–3, 31–2
moral character trait *see* Aristotle virtue
mom's *sopapillas* 54
mosh pit 73

Nacho Libre 29
nice 69

Picard, Jean-Luc 70
Plato 1, 9–10, 59n28
paradox 43, 71, 89n29
philosophy 84–5
play: conflicting views 43–5; connection to leisure in Aristotle 11; connection to morality 82; connection to pleasure in Aristotle 19; connection to temperance in Aristotle 21–2; definitions 56–57n2; empirical science of 5, 45–56; Greek words for 11; gender differences 55; Heraclitus vs. Plato 9–10; human vs. non-human 49–53; in non-humans 45–9; moral stakes of 66–70; political importance 50–4; as part of happiness for Aristotle 17, 39–41; as *pharmakon* for Aristotle 11, 25; as restful 12; uses of value in human forms 5–6; vs. playfulness 2, 30
playfulness 70–86; attributes of 6, 30, 70–81; and creativity vs. rigidity and unruliness 72, 77; as crucial for life 85–6, 93–4; definition 3–6, 41, 64, 66–7, 70–81, 93; and emotions and moods 71–2; and humility vs. fragility and recklessness 77–8; necessity for happiness 3, 6, 81–6; and optimism vs. naïveté 78–9; and philosophy 84–5; psychology of 70–2; and relaxation and unselfing 72–5; and seriousness vs. flakiness and severity 75–7; and sociality 79–81; versus play 2
Polyphia 71
poop and pee 50, 59n33

queer spaces 52, 69

rest 6, 66, 72–5

scholē see leisure
shitposting 67
spoilsport 77
spontaneity 72–3
sports 7, 12, 51–2, 90n45
Star Trek 15, 68

tag *see* you
tavern 6, 51–2, 69
third places 51
time affluence 73
ToeJam and Earl 30

unselfing 73–4

virtue ethics 4, 29

you *see* it

For Product Safety Concerns and Information please contact our EU
representative GPSR@taylorandfrancis.com
Taylor & Francis Verlag GmbH, Kaufingerstraße 24, 80331 München, Germany

www.ingramcontent.com/pod-product-compliance
Lightning Source LLC
Chambersburg PA
CBHW051756230426
43670CB00012B/2309